Whip Me, Beat Me, Make My Heart Your Own:

The Loving BDSM Couples Handbook

Written by Ald
Published by Dizzy-Angel Multimedia

Whip Me, Beat Me, Make My Heart Your Own: The Loving BDSM Couples Handbook
Copyright © 2024 Studio Apophis
All rights reserved.

No part of this book may be reproduced, distributed, or transmitted in any form or by any means, including photocopying, recording, or other electronic or mechanical methods, without the prior written permission of the publisher, except in the case of brief quotations embodied in critical reviews and specific other noncommercial uses permitted by copyright law.

Published by Dizzy-Angel Multimedia

First Edition

<u>Contents</u>

A Note to the Seekers

Welcome to those who have opened this book with curiosity, courage, or longing. You are part of a unique community of seekers who yearn for deeper connections, richer experiences, and a fuller understanding of living and loving authentically.

This journey is not for the faint of heart. It is for those who understand that true pleasure often comes with vulnerability and that trust is the foundation of all meaningful connections.

To those who find exhilaration in the mix of pleasure and pain, you are not broken. You are beautifully attuned to the intricate ways our hearts and bodies communicate. To explore this path is to celebrate your capacity to feel deeply, to trust openly, and to find meaning in places others might never venture.

For those who wish to understand, know this: the world of BDSM is not just about actions—it's about the emotions, trust, and care that underlie them. It's about finding joy in the balance between control and surrender, strength and vulnerability, and giving and receiving.

You are brave enough to seek more from life. Whether you are a seasoned participant in this dynamic, a curious explorer, or someone fascinated by the kaleidoscope of human desire, this book is here to honor your journey.

So, take a deep breath, open your mind, and step forward. What lies ahead is not just a guide—it's a celebration of trust, love, and the courage to be yourself in every way.

You are seen, valid, and worthy of the connections and experiences you seek.

With love,
Ald

Before the First Strike: A Foundation of Trust and Care

Welcome to the world of BDSM, a realm of connection, exploration, and trust that many find both intriguing and misunderstood. The acronym itself—**Bondage & Discipline, Dominance & Submission, Sadism & Masochism**—might conjure up dramatic imagery. Still, BDSM is far more than the stereotypes that often define it in popular culture. It is a profoundly personal and multifaceted lifestyle rooted in respect, consent, and the shared journey of self-discovery.

At its core, BDSM offers a unique way to explore the interplay of power, vulnerability, and sensation within human relationships. For some, it's a playful extension of intimacy. For others, it's a deeply ingrained part of their identity. The beauty of BDSM lies in its vast spectrum—there's no "one-size-fits-all" approach. Whether someone engages in light bondage or embarks on an all-encompassing Dominant/submissive relationship, every dynamic is valid as long as it is consensual and fulfilling for all involved.

However, BDSM remains shrouded in misconceptions. Some believe it is synonymous with abuse or assume it's all about physical pain. These ideas couldn't be further from the truth. BDSM is about **choice**, not harm. It's about exploring what makes us feel alive, connected, and accessible. For many, it provides a safe and structured way to delve into the emotions and sensations society often tells us to suppress.

Within the BDSM lifestyle, there is a strong emphasis on safety and informed participation. Those who practice BDSM often speak of "safe, sane, and consensual" or "risk-aware consensual kink" as guiding principles. These concepts underscore the thoughtfulness that goes into crafting experiences that are physically safe and emotionally respectful.

Finally, BDSM is deeply personal. It is not about fitting into a predefined mold but discovering what speaks to your heart, body, and mind. For some, it's about relinquishing control and finding freedom in submission. For others, it's about embracing the responsibility of leadership as a Dominant. And for many, it's about the trust, communication, and intimacy that underpin these dynamics.

BDSM is not just about what happens in the bedroom or dungeon. It's a philosophy of connection and exploration. Whether you are new to this world or looking to deepen your understanding, remember you are not alone. This book guides you to walk this path with confidence, compassion, and curiosity.

BDSM is often misunderstood, and that's not surprising, given how it's portrayed in media and pop culture. To truly grasp what BDSM is, it's crucial to peel back the layers of misconception and look at its foundation.

At its heart, BDSM is about **choice, trust, and consent**. It is an intentional exploration of power dynamics, sensations, and relationships that defy the mainstream notions of intimacy. It offers practitioners a unique way to connect—not just physically but emotionally and psychologically—with their partners and, often, with themselves.

What BDSM Is

1. **A Framework for Connection**
    BDSM relationships are built on open communication, mutual respect, and
    shared understanding. They provide a structured way to explore intimacy
    through playful experimentation or deeply committed dynamics. For many,
    they're a way to express love and affection through rituals, roles, and acts that
    hold profound meaning.

2. **An Avenue for Exploration**
    BDSM is not just about physical sensations but emotional and psychological
    discovery. It allows individuals to explore their desires, boundaries, and fears
    safely. Many practitioners describe the experience as liberating, clarifying
    their needs and identities.

3. **Deeply Personal and Unique**
    No two BDSM relationships are the same. While some couples enjoy light
    bondage or playful teasing, others embrace intense power exchanges or
    specific fetishes. What matters is that the arrangement is satisfying and
    consensual for all parties involved.

4. **Rooted in Trust and Consent**
    Central to BDSM is the idea that **everything is negotiated and agreed upon**.
    Safe words, boundaries, and aftercare ensure everyone feels secure and
    respected. It's not about imposing will or causing harm—crafting experiences
    that bring joy, release, and connection.

What BDSM Isn't

1. **Abuse or Coercion**
    One of the most damaging myths about BDSM is that it's abusive. In truth,
    BDSM is the opposite of coercion. It requires clear communication,
    enthusiastic consent, and ongoing dialogue. Any violation of these principles
    is not BDSM—it's abuse.

2. **Only About Pain or Sex**
    While BDSM often involves physical sensations, it is not synonymous with
    pain. Many practitioners never engage in sadomasochism at all. Similarly,
    BDSM doesn't have to involve sex—it can be about psychological
    connection, emotional fulfillment, or power dynamics unrelated to physical
    intimacy.

3. **A Quick Thrill**
    For many, BDSM is not just a "kink" or fleeting interest—it's an integral part
    of their identity or relationship dynamic. It requires effort, communication,
    and care to navigate successfully.

4. **For Everyone**
    While BDSM can offer profound rewards, it's not for everyone. Some people
    might not resonate with its principles or practices, and that's okay. There's no
    "right" way to love or connect—what matters is that you honor your truth.

Reframing the Narrative

Understanding BDSM requires an open mind and a willingness to question
assumptions. It's not about what society tells us intimacy should look like—it's about
creating a framework that honors the unique needs, desires, and boundaries of everyone
involved.

By dispelling the myths and focusing on the values that define BDSM, we can
better appreciate the depth, beauty, and potential it holds.

BDSM is rooted in values that ensure safety, respect, and mutual fulfillment.
These values—**consent, communication, and care**—act as the pillars that support
healthy and enriching dynamics. While the acts might appear unconventional, the
principles governing them universally apply to any intimate relationship.

Consent: The Bedrock of Trust

Consent is non-negotiable in BDSM. Every interaction, whether physical touch, power
exchange, or emotional vulnerability, must be based on explicit, enthusiastic, and
informed agreement. Unlike in many "vanilla" relationships, where assumptions may
sometimes replace explicit discussions, BDSM practitioners emphasize intentional and
ongoing consent.

Negotiation Before Action

Before any scene or dynamic begins, participants discuss their boundaries, desires,
and expectations. This negotiation establishes a shared understanding of what will
happen and ensures everyone feels safe and heard.

Safe Words and Signals

To maintain consent throughout an activity, participants use safe words or signals that
allow them to pause or stop the interaction at any time. These tools ensure that no one
feels trapped or powerless.

Enthusiastic, Not Obligatory

Consent in BDSM is always enthusiastic and freely given. It's never coerced,
pressured, or assumed. The principle of "no means no" is absolute, but equally
important is the idea that "yes" can be withdrawn at any moment.

Communication: The Lifeline of Connection

BDSM thrives on **radical honesty**. Open, transparent dialogue allows participants to
understand each other's needs, boundaries, and experiences, creating a foundation of
trust.

Discussing Desires and Boundaries
Before engaging in BDSM, partners openly discuss their fantasies, limits, and triggers. This conversation often reveals vulnerabilities and desires that might otherwise remain hidden, deepening intimacy.**Ongoing Check-Ins**
Communication doesn't end once an activity begins. During a scene, participants may check in with each other to ensure everyone is comfortable and enjoying the experience. Afterward, debriefing or aftercare conversations help process emotions and reinforce the connection.

Non-Judgmental Listening
Partners create a safe space to share without fear of judgment. This openness fosters more profound understanding and encourages growth within the relationship.

Care: The Heart of BDSM

Despite its edgy reputation, BDSM is deeply caring. Practitioners are often exceptionally attuned to their partner's emotional and physical well-being. Care ensures that every interaction is grounded in love and respect, whether through aftercare, attentiveness during scenes, or showing appreciation outside of play.

Physical Safety
Practitioners take steps to minimize risks by educating themselves about their activities, using proper equipment, and understanding the human body's limits.

Emotional Support
Many BDSM activities evoke strong emotions, from euphoria to vulnerability. Partners provide reassurance, comfort, and support during and after scenes to help process these feelings.

Celebrating Connection
Care is also about honoring the bond between partners. Whether through a small gesture of gratitude or an act of service, showing care reinforces the mutual respect that underpins BDSM.

Living the Values

By prioritizing consent, communication, and care, BDSM practitioners create spaces where vulnerability becomes strength, boundaries become opportunities for connection, and trust becomes the cornerstone of every interaction. These values are not just guidelines—they are a way of life for those who practice BDSM with love, respect, and authenticity.

BDSM often exists on the fringes of mainstream understanding, shrouded in stereotypes and misconceptions. These misunderstandings can create unnecessary fear, shame, or judgment for those curious about exploring the lifestyle. Dispelling these myths is an essential step toward appreciating BDSM as a practice rooted in consent, trust, and emotional depth.

Myth 1: BDSM Is Abusive or Violent

One of the most persistent misconceptions is that BDSM is synonymous with abuse. The reality is the opposite: abuse is non-consensual, harmful, and destructive, while BDSM is consensual, respectful, and collaborative. Every act within BDSM, even those that mimic pain or control, is rooted in mutual agreement and trust.

- Abuse removes power; BDSM is about sharing or exchanging power in ways both partners agree upon.

- While outsiders might see and misinterpret a scene, practitioners understand that every action has been carefully negotiated, no matter how intense.

- Far from being harmful, BDSM can be healing and empowering for those involved.

Myth 2: BDSM Is All About Sex

While sexual elements often play a role, BDSM is not inherently about sex. For many participants, the experience is more about emotional intimacy, power dynamics, or personal exploration than physical gratification.

- A dominant partner might feel fulfilled by providing structure and guidance, while a submissive partner might find comfort in surrendering control.

- Some scenes or relationships are entirely non-sexual, focusing instead on trust, creativity, or emotional connection.

Myth 3: BDSM Practitioners Are Damaged or Deviant

Another harmful stereotype is that people who engage in BDSM must be broken, traumatized, or abnormal. This myth stems from a lack of understanding and societal taboos around pleasure and pain.

- Studies show that BDSM practitioners often have higher levels of communication skills, emotional intelligence, and self-awareness.

- Many people who engage in BDSM are well-adjusted individuals who embrace unconventional forms of intimacy.

Myth 4: BDSM Always Involves Extreme Activities

When people think of BDSM, they often picture extreme scenarios involving heavy bondage, intense pain, or elaborate roleplays. BDSM exists on a spectrum, and every practitioner defines their comfort level.

- For some, BDSM might involve light spanking, playful teasing, or gentle restraint.

- For others, it could mean exploring intricate power dynamics without physical activities.

Myth 5: The Dominant Partner Has All the Power

A common misunderstanding is that dominants dictate every aspect of the relationship or scene without regard for the submissive's wishes. In truth, BDSM is about mutual exchange, with both partners holding equal responsibility and power in different ways.

- The submissive often sets the boundaries and limits, which the dominant respects.

- The dynamic thrives on collaboration, not unilateral control.

Myth 6: BDSM Is Shameful or Immoral

Cultural and religious taboos often paint BDSM as something to hide or feel ashamed of. However, practitioners know their lifestyle is as valid and beautiful as any other form of love or intimacy when practiced with care and consent.

- Many people find liberation and self-expression in BDSM, celebrating their individuality and desires.

- Morality is subjective, and what matters most is that all involved act respectfully and kindly toward each other.

Myth 7: BDSM Is Easy to Understand Through Mainstream Media

Popular portrayals of BDSM, such as those in certain books or movies, often misrepresent the lifestyle by focusing on drama, danger, or unrealistic scenarios. These depictions can be entertaining but are rarely accurate.

- BDSM in real life is less about spectacle and more about thoughtful exploration.

- Practitioners learn, practice, and build trust before engaging in activities.

Breaking Down Barriers

Understanding the truths of BDSM helps create a more accepting and compassionate world. By dispelling myths, we not only validate the experiences of those who practice BDSM but also invite others to explore their desires without fear or judgment.

Consent is the cornerstone of BDSM. Without it, BDSM is no different from abuse. What sets BDSM apart from violence or assault is the explicit, enthusiastic, and ongoing agreement between all parties involved. Consent within the BDSM community is multifaceted, involving clear communication, mutual respect, and the continuous negotiation of boundaries.

Informed Consent

Informed consent means that all participants are fully aware of what the experience will entail. It's not just about agreeing to participate but understanding the nature of the scene, the roles, the risks, and the limits. Everyone involved must know precisely what they're signing up for, emotionally and physically.

Clear Communication: Before engaging in any BDSM activity, all parties should discuss their expectations, interests, boundaries, and hard limits.

Knowledge of Risks: Every activity carries some risk, no matter how light or intense. Partners should communicate potential dangers, including physical, emotional, and psychological.

Revocation of Consent: Consent can be withdrawn at any time; all parties must know this. A safe word or signal should be established beforehand to stop the scene immediately if things become uncomfortable.

Negotiation and Boundaries

One of the most critical aspects of BDSM is the negotiation process, where all participants set clear boundaries. This can cover anything from specific activities to emotional triggers. Setting boundaries isn't just about listing things you don't want to do; it's about creating a space where everyone feels safe and respected.

Hard Limits: These are activities or situations that are off-limits, regardless of the context. For example, a hard limit might include certain impact plays or psychological scenarios.

Soft Limits: These boundaries might be negotiable or change depending on the partner, environment, or context. They could involve specific activities that are a "maybe" but should always be communicated clearly.

Continual Negotiation: Consent doesn't just happen once before the scene. It is an ongoing conversation, both during and after the experience. As people's emotional and physical states change, so too should the negotiation of consent.

The Role of the Safe Word

A safe word is a vital tool in any BDSM scene, serving as a quick and straightforward way for a participant to communicate their comfort level. When a participant uses the safe word, the activity should stop immediately. Safe words ensure that the scene remains consensual and allow the participants to feel confident that their needs and limits will be respected.

Common Safe Words: "Red" and "Yellow" are widely recognized in the BDSM community. "Red" means stop immediately, while "Yellow" signals that the person needs to slow down or adjust the intensity.

Non-Verbal Safe Words: In situations where verbal communication may not be possible (e.g., gagging or restraints), non-verbal cues, such as tapping or snapping fingers, can substitute.

Aftercare: Caring for the Mind and Body

Aftercare is checking in with your partner after a scene, ensuring they feel safe, cared for, and grounded. BDSM can trigger strong emotional or physical reactions; aftercare is essential for emotional healing and reassurance. It also helps partners return to balance, especially after intense scenes.

Physical Care: This could involve helping your partner hydrate, offering a blanket, or tending to any physical marks or bruises.

Emotional Care: BDSM can stir up deep emotions, so aftercare might also involve offering comfort, validation, and emotional support. This is the time for partners to debrief and discuss the experience, affirming their connection and trust.

The Ethical Considerations of Consent

The ethics of consent in BDSM are grounded in the belief that all participants should feel empowered to make their own choices without fear of pressure or manipulation. Consent should always be given freely, enthusiastically, and without coercion. Consent is never assumed—it is always explicitly communicated and continuously respected.

Avoiding Coercion: While the dynamics of dominance and submission can involve power exchange, the dominant partner should never use their position to coerce or manipulate the submissive into something they don't want to do.

Mutual Responsibility: Consent is not just the responsibility of the dominant partner—it's a mutual responsibility. The submissive partner must communicate their limits and desires just as clearly as the dominant partner. Both parties should be willing to stop if consent is withdrawn or someone feels unsafe.

The Power of 'No'

In BDSM, saying "no" is just as important as saying "yes." A participant's ability to set clear limits and boundaries enhances the experience for everyone involved. When someone says "no," their word should be respected without question, and it should never be interpreted as part of the roleplay or scene unless explicitly agreed upon in advance.

Empowerment in Saying No: The ability to refuse or stop an activity at any time enhances trust and deepens the emotional connection between participants.

No Means No: In all aspects of BDSM, the phrase "no means no" should always be the guiding principle. It's a protective measure that ensures everyone feels heard and respected.

Trust and Respect as the Foundation of Consent

Consent is not only about communication—it's about trust. In BDSM, trust is a vital component that allows participants to explore their desires safely and deeply. For consent to be meaningful, it must be built on mutual respect. Both parties should feel safe and secure in their boundaries and their ability to communicate openly.

Trust Between Partners: The emotional bond that grows between participants in BDSM is rooted in trust. This trust allows people to explore vulnerabilities, experiment with power dynamics, and confidently engage in intense or intimate activities.

Respect for Boundaries: True consent means respecting verbal and non-verbal cues. It's not just about checking off activities on a list but about honoring the space each participant needs to feel secure and empowered.

Communication is the bedrock of any healthy BDSM relationship. Without it, the complex dynamics of power exchange, trust, and intimacy would crumble. Whether it's verbal or non-verbal, effective communication ensures that all parties involved feel seen, heard, and respected. In the world of BDSM, communication is not only about expressing needs and desires but also about understanding boundaries, fears, and limits.

The Basics of Clear Communication

Clear communication is essential in all relationships, but in BDSM, it becomes even more crucial. The power dynamics in BDSM—where one partner assumes a dominant role and the other a submissive role—require a high level of understanding between participants. Without constant, open dialogue, misunderstandings and missteps can occur, potentially leading to discomfort, harm, or emotional distress.

Discussing Desires: Before engaging in any scene, both partners should openly discuss their desires, what they hope to get out of the experience, and any specific fantasies they want to explore. For example, a submissive may wish to explore humiliation play, while the dominant may prefer to experiment with impact play. These desires must be communicated in advance to ensure everyone's on the same page.

Establishing Boundaries: Setting clear boundaries is one of the most critical aspects of communication. Boundaries define what is acceptable and what is not and help keep everyone safe. The dominant and submissive must clearly express their hard limits (things they do not want to do) and soft limits (things they might be open to under certain circumstances).

Active Listening: Communication in BDSM is a two-way street. Both partners must practice active listening, entirely focusing on what the other person is saying and responding thoughtfully. This involves hearing the words and interpreting the emotional and nonverbal cues behind them. Active listening helps build empathy and strengthens the emotional connection between partners.

Verbal Communication in BDSM

While some BDSM play may incorporate non-verbal cues, verbal communication is still vital, particularly when it comes to negotiating scenes, establishing trust, and checking in during aftercare. The words exchanged between a dominant and submissive set the tone, establish boundaries, and ensure that everything is consensual and understood.

Pre-Scene Negotiation: Before a scene begins, it's essential to have a detailed conversation about what will happen. What activities are on the table? What are the boundaries? Is there any "safe word" or non-verbal cue in place? Setting the stage through detailed verbal communication will ensure the scene progresses smoothly and safely.

Safe Words and Cues: As mentioned earlier, a safe word is an essential tool in BDSM. However, verbal communication during the scene doesn't stop there. The dominant partner should regularly check in with the submissive, asking if they're still comfortable or if anything needs to be adjusted. Communicating openly within the scene is essential, whether through affirmations ("Are you okay?") or using agreed-upon phrases to slow down or stop the scene if necessary.

The Power of "No": "No" is a word that is powerful in BDSM, as it signifies a boundary that should be respected. However, it's essential to understand that "no" may not always mean "stop" in the context of specific BDSM dynamics. Some submissives may want to engage in certain forms of roleplay where "no" is part of the script. In these cases, both partners should understand what it means in that specific context and always respect the power of the word outside of agreed-upon scenarios.

Non-verbal Communication in BDSM

BDSM often involves power exchange, where one partner may have more control over the other. Despite this power differential, nonverbal communication is just as important as verbal communication—if not more so. Body language, facial expressions, and physical cues all play an integral role in guiding and shaping the scene.

Reading Body Language: The dominant partner should always observe the submissive's body language to assess their emotional and physical state. Subtle signs of discomfort or hesitation—such as flinching, tense muscles, or a shift in posture—should be noticed and acted upon immediately.

Physical Cues: Physical cues can occur if verbal communication isn't possible. This could be as simple as tapping out, making eye contact, or using hand signals to indicate discomfort or the need to stop. Non-verbal cues allow both parties to communicate without breaking the flow of the scene.

Facial Expressions: A submissive's facial expressions can often provide insight into their feelings, and the dominant partner should remain attuned to these. A smile or a wink might indicate joy and engagement, while a grimace or tears may signal something wrong. Being able to read these expressions helps maintain a safe and consensual atmosphere.

Ongoing Communication in BDSM

Communication in BDSM doesn't end when the scene is over. The dynamic between the dominant and submissive partners continues after the scene with debriefing, aftercare, and continued conversation. This ongoing dialogue ensures that both parties feel heard, respected, and validated throughout the experience.

Debriefing: After a scene, both participants should engage in a debriefing session, discussing how things went, what worked, and what could be improved. This is not a time for judgment but for constructive feedback that strengthens the relationship and enhances future experiences.

Aftercare Conversations: Aftercare isn't just about physical comfort; it's also about emotional reassurance. It's an opportunity for the dominant and submissive to check in with each other, offering comfort and care. Even a simple "How are you feeling?" can show deep care and attentiveness to the submissive's emotional needs.

Continuing the Conversation: As relationships evolve, so will desires, limits, and dynamics. BDSM partners must keep the lines of communication open, checking in regularly with each other to ensure that everyone is on the same page. This means revisiting past conversations about desires and boundaries to ensure that the relationship continues to grow in a safe and healthy direction.

The Role of Communication in Building Trust

Trust is perhaps the most critical foundation in BDSM relationships, and effective communication is the key to building and maintaining that trust. When both partners feel that they can communicate openly and honestly, it creates a sense of security that makes it easier to explore the deeper aspects of BDSM. When communication is clear, both parties are more likely to take emotional and physical risks because they know they are being heard and their limits will be respected.

Building Emotional Intimacy: Open communication in BDSM leads to emotional intimacy. As partners express their desires, fears, and boundaries, they share more than just physical experiences—they share parts of their inner worlds. This mutual vulnerability can strengthen the emotional bond between the dominant and submissive.

Reaffirming Trust: Trust is built over time through consistent and respectful communication. As partners continually engage in honest dialogue, they reaffirm their commitment to one another, making the BDSM dynamic more fulfilling and connected.

Communication and Conflict Resolution

No relationship is free from conflict, and BDSM relationships are no exception. However, how conflict is handled is critical in maintaining trust and safety. In BDSM, disagreements or discomforts should be addressed respectfully and with care.

Acknowledging Discomfort: If a participant feels uncomfortable or violated during a scene or afterward, it's essential to address the issue immediately. This doesn't mean "blaming" the dominant partner but instead sharing feelings and concerns so the relationship can grow and adapt.

Resolving Issues with Respect: Communication is critical to resolving conflicts. Both partners should express their feelings calmly and respectfully, understanding that conflict doesn't mean the end of the relationship—it's an opportunity for growth and understanding.

Aftercare is one of the most vital yet often overlooked components of BDSM play. While the intensity of a scene can be exhilarating, the emotional and physical needs of both the dominant and submissive must be addressed afterward to ensure well-being, trust, and care. Aftercare is checking in, comforting, and reassuring your partner once the scene has ended. It's a time to bridge the emotional gap between the end of an intense experience and the return to everyday life.

Why Aftercare Matters

BDSM scenes—especially those involving intense play, power dynamics, or deep emotional vulnerability—can leave participants feeling emotionally and physically drained. Aftercare allows both partners to transition back to a more neutral emotional state and helps ensure that the play doesn't negatively affect their well-being. Aftercare isn't just for the submissive; it is an essential practice for the dominant as well. Both individuals are emotionally involved, and their needs must be considered.

Emotional Impact: Intense BDSM play can invoke a range of emotions, from joy and excitement to vulnerability and even post-play "subdrop" (a temporary emotional slump that can occur after a scene). For submissives, aftercare is crucial to help process those emotions. It's equally essential for dominants to offer reassurance and check in with their partner to ensure that both parties are emotionally stable.

Physical Impact: Many BDSM activities, such as impact play or bondage, can leave the body sore, bruised, or physically drained. Aftercare includes physical care, like soothing touches, warm blankets, and hydration. For both the dominant and the submissive, tending to the body's needs after a scene helps with recovery.

What Aftercare Looks Like

Aftercare is highly personalized and can look different from one relationship or scene to the next. Some partners may need a quiet moment of solitude to process their experience, while others may want comforting touch, reassurance, or words of affirmation. Regardless of the specifics, aftercare is about showing your partner that their emotional and physical needs are important to you.

Physical Care: The submissive or dominant might require physical care depending on the scene. This could involve offering a blanket, gently removing restraints, applying soothing lotions or oils to bruised skin, or simply holding your partner to provide warmth.

Words of Comfort and Reassurance: After intense BDSM scenes, it's common for both participants to need verbal reassurances. The dominant might offer praise or reassurance, letting the submissive know they were safe, desired, and appreciated. This can help rebuild a sense of security and trust. The submissive may also want to express their feelings; the dominant should listen and offer comfort.

Emotional Reassurance: For some submissives, aftercare might mean receiving praise for their obedience and vulnerability during the scene. For the dominant, it can mean reassurance that they have cared for their submissive's well-being throughout the experience. A dominant should always check in to see how the submissive feels emotionally and what they need. This helps prevent emotional distress or feelings of abandonment.

The Dynamics of Aftercare for Dominants

While aftercare is often associated with the submissive partner, dominants also require care after an intense scene. The emotional toll on a dominant can be just as significant as on a submissive, even if it manifests differently. For the dominant, aftercare provides an opportunity to ensure that they feel grounded and emotionally secure after a robust control exchange.

Recognizing the Dominant's Needs: Aftercare for the dominant may not be as physically demanding, but it can still be emotionally fulfilling. The dominant may need a moment to decompress, to celebrate their success in guiding their partner, or to process the emotional energy spent during the scene.

Reaffirming the Bond: Aftercare also allows the dominant and submissive to reaffirm their emotional bond. This is when they can openly express gratitude and appreciation for each other. The dominant might express pride in their submissive for having trusted them, while the submissive might express appreciation for the care and consideration given.

Supporting Emotional Vulnerability: Many dominants are highly attuned to their submissive's emotional states, but they too can feel vulnerable after a scene. The submissive must offer support and reaffirm their trust in the dominant. This mutual vulnerability deepens the emotional connection and fortifies the trust between the two partners.

Creating a Personalized Aftercare Plan

Aftercare should be tailored to the unique needs of both the dominant and submissive. This can be done by communicating beforehand what type of aftercare each person requires and creating a plan. This allows the scene to end with mutual respect and reassurance, preventing post-scene confusion or emotional fallout.

Discuss Preferences Beforehand: Before engaging in a BDSM scene, both parties must discuss their aftercare needs. The submissive might prefer physical touch, while the dominant may require emotional grounding. Setting these expectations ahead of time ensures a smoother transition once the scene ends.

Flexibility in Aftercare: While having a plan is necessary, it's also essential to remain flexible. Sometimes, a submissive may need more comfort than anticipated, or a dominant may need more time to process their feelings. Communicating throughout the aftercare process ensures that both partners feel secure in their emotional and physical needs.

Adjusting Aftercare Based on the Scene: The type of aftercare required might change depending on the scene's intensity. For example, after a high-intensity impact scene, a submissive may need more physical touch and attention to soreness, while after a psychological scene, they may need more emotional reassurance.

The Long-Term Impact of Aftercare

Consistent, thoughtful aftercare helps solidify trust and emotional connection in the long term. Aftercare can strengthen the bond and foster growth in the relationship by ensuring that both partners' physical and emotional needs are met. It also serves as a reminder that BDSM is not just about the physical acts but about the deep emotional and psychological connections that are formed between partners.

Aftercare Beyond the Scene

Finally, aftercare doesn't end when the scene is over. Aftercare is about the ongoing emotional care and support given to one another throughout the BDSM journey. This might involve continued communication in the days following the scene, checking in with each other, and ensuring that both partners feel seen, valued, and supported as they navigate their shared dynamic.

A Loving Perspective: Respect, Empowerment, and Curiosity

At its heart, BDSM is not just about the acts, the roles, or even the tools—it is about the profound human connections that arise from mutual trust, understanding, and love. Far from being cold or detached, BDSM offers a unique opportunity to express love and care in ways that honor the individuality of each partner.

Respect and Empowerment

The foundation of any successful BDSM dynamic is mutual respect. Dominants and submissives are equal partners in the dance of power exchange, each contributing their unique desires, vulnerabilities, and strengths. While their roles may differ, their importance is always balanced.

For Dominants: Respect means valuing the trust and vulnerability the submissive offers. It is an honor to be entrusted with someone's body, emotions, and boundaries, and true dominance is about empowerment, not exploitation.

For Submissives: Respect involves recognizing the effort and care a dominant provides. Submissives empower their partners to lead with confidence and compassion by giving their trust.

BDSM is a shared journey where partners lift each other, celebrating their roles and humanity.

Celebrating Diversity

The world of BDSM is as diverse as the people who participate in it. From soft, sensual dominance to intense impact play, from elaborate roleplays to simple acts of submission, the lifestyle offers countless ways to connect, explore, and grow. This diversity is a strength—it reminds us that no two relationships are the same and that there is no single "right" way to experience BDSM.

This inclusivity extends to the people within the community as well. Regardless of gender, orientation, or experience level, BDSM welcomes all who approach it with respect and curiosity. It is a space where differences are celebrated and individuality is honored.

An Invitation to the Curious

If you are new to BDSM or exploring it for the first time, let this serve as an invitation to approach it with an open mind, an open heart, and a spirit of curiosity. There is no need to have all the answers or to fit into predefined roles. Instead, give yourself permission to explore, learn, and grow.

BDSM is not about perfection—it's about connection. It's about finding joy in the journey, discovering the parts of yourself you didn't know existed, and deepening the bond with your partner. Whether you are here to learn about the lifestyle, expand your horizons, or understand others better, know there is no judgment, only support for your journey.

In the end, BDSM is a celebration of the human capacity to connect deeply, live authentically, and embrace the full spectrum of pleasure and trust. It is not just a lifestyle; it is an act of courage and a testament to the beauty of human relationships.

So, step into this world with respect, empowerment, and curiosity. You may find that what you discover about yourself and others is more meaningful than ever imagined.

The Dom

The Dominant Partner

In any healthy power exchange dynamic, the dominant role is one of profound responsibility and care. Dominance is not about exerting control for the sake of power; it's about understanding the balance between strength and sensitivity and how that balance can nurture deep, mutual trust. As a Dominant, you guide your partner through vulnerability, growth, and exploration. Your role is not to overpower but to empower, creating a space where you and your partner can thrive together in the fullness of your dynamic.

True dominance is rooted in respect, wisdom, and compassion. It's about providing structure and guidance while knowing your partner's emotional and physical needs. A skilled Dominant understands that their power comes from the ability to create safety, trust, and clarity within the relationship, allowing the submissive to surrender with confidence and openness. It is your responsibility to ensure that your partner's physical and emotional safety is prioritized while simultaneously cultivating an environment where both of you can explore and evolve.

The exercises in this section will encourage you to reflect on what it means to be a Dominant and explore how your actions, decisions, and energy shape the dynamic. They will challenge you to examine how to wield your power with intention, awareness, and care and to find balance in your leadership. You will be asked to look within—better to understand your desires, limits, and boundaries—and reflect on how these elements shape your relationship.

Dominance is not about asserting control over another person; it's about creating a partnership where both individuals feel seen, heard, and valued. The strength of a true Dominant lies in the ability to serve the dynamic with integrity, consistency, and a deep commitment to the relationship and your partner's well-being.

As you engage with these meditations, practices, and journaling exercises, remember that this journey is not just about asserting power—it is about refining your ability to lead with wisdom and care and enhancing the emotional and physical connection you share. By stepping fully into your role, you create a dynamic where you and your partner can discover more profound layers of trust, intimacy, and fulfillment.

The Foundation of Trust

Meditation:

Find a quiet, comfortable place to sit or lie down. Please close your eyes and take a deep breath, letting it fill your lungs. Hold it for a moment, then exhale slowly, releasing any tension in your body. Repeat this process until you feel calm and centered.

Now, visualize trust as a strong, unshakable bridge connecting you and your partner. Imagine the materials it's made of—perhaps steel, wood, or stone. Notice how each element represents the foundation of your dynamic: honesty, vulnerability, communication, and respect.

Picture yourself walking across this bridge, feeling its strength beneath your feet. With each step, remind yourself of the trust you've built together. Reflect on the moments that solidified this bond—the times you've listened without judgment, offered reassurance or stayed true to your word.

Let gratitude fill your heart for the trust you've cultivated. Recognize that trust is a growing entity that requires care and intention. With every breath, I feel the bridge becoming even more robust, capable of withstanding anything life brings.

Affirmation: **I honor the trust I share with my partner. It is the foundation of our connection and a testament to our mutual respect and love.**

Practices in Action:

- **Activity 1: Consent and Boundaries Check-In**
  Set aside dedicated time to review your dynamic's boundaries, limits, and agreements with your partner. Use this to update your consent checklist, ensuring it reflects your current needs and desires. Approach this practice with openness and honesty, valuing each other's input equally.
  Tip: Frame this conversation as a shared commitment to growth rather than an obligation.

- **Activity 2: Gratitude Exercise**
  Take a moment to write a letter to your partner expressing gratitude for the trust you share. Highlight specific instances where they've demonstrated reliability, care, or understanding. Share the letter if you feel comfortable, or keep it as a reminder of the strength of your bond.
  Tip: Invite your partner to write their letter if you feel inspired.

Journaling Prompt:

1. What does trust mean to me in this relationship?

2. How does trust feel in my body and emotions—calm, safe, secure?

3. Reflect on a moment when trust deepened between me and my partner. What happened, and why did it have such an impact?

Closing Reflection:

Take a deep breath, letting the reflection settle into your heart and mind. Trust is a gift, a cornerstone of any meaningful relationship. As you move forward, carry this meditation with you, nurturing the trust you've built and allowing it to grow even more profound.

Remember, trust isn't about perfection—it's about showing up for each other, again and again, with love and intention. Committing to trust creates a space where vulnerability is met with safety, and love can flourish.

You and your partner are worthy of trust. Together, you build something beautiful and enduring.

Personal Reflections:

Exploring Vulnerability

Meditation:

Begin by sitting or lying comfortably somewhere you feel safe and undisturbed. Close your eyes and take a slow, deep breath, inhaling through your nose and exhaling through your mouth. Repeat this a few times, letting your body relax with each exhale.

Once calm, bring your attention inward. Reflect on what vulnerability means to you. Think about times you've allowed yourself to be open—emotionally, mentally, or physically. How did it feel? Was it freeing, terrifying, or perhaps a mix of both?

Picture vulnerability as a doorway in your mind. On one side is the fear of being exposed or judged; on the other is the deep connection and understanding that vulnerability makes possible. See yourself stepping through that doorway. As you pass through, you leave fear behind and embrace the courage that comes from being authentic and open.

Now, visualize your partner waiting on the other side of the doorway. Imagine sharing a part of yourself with them—something you've held back. Picture their response, meeting your vulnerability with kindness and acceptance.

Sit with this image momentarily, allowing a sense of empowerment to grow. Remind yourself that vulnerability is not weakness; it's a testament to your strength and willingness to deepen your bond.

Affirmation: **I honor my vulnerability as a pathway to connection and growth. By embracing it, I strengthen myself and my relationship.**

Practices in Action:

- **Activity 1: Sharing a Vulnerability**
  Choose one emotional or physical vulnerability you haven't yet shared with your partner. This could be a fear, an experience, or even a boundary you find difficult to articulate. Schedule a quiet, intentional moment to share this with your partner, framing it as an opportunity to deepen your connection.
  Tip: Use "I" statements to express your feelings without fear of judgment. For example: *"I feel nervous sharing this, but I trust you to listen without judgment."*

- **Activity 2: Receiving Vulnerability with Care**
  Invite your partner to share something vulnerable with you in return. Practice active listening, giving them your full attention without interrupting. Respond with empathy and gratitude, letting them know you value their openness.
  Tip: Avoid trying to "fix" or problem-solve. Sometimes, just listening and acknowledging their feelings is enough.

Journaling Prompt:

1. What does vulnerability mean to me in my relationship? How has it shaped my dynamic with my partner?

2. Reflect on a time when you allowed yourself to be vulnerable. How did it feel, and what did you learn from the experience?

3. How has embracing vulnerability with my partner strengthened our trust and connection?

Closing Reflection:

Take a moment to breathe deeply, letting the reflection settle in your mind. Vulnerability is not easy—it requires courage, trust, and self-awareness. By embracing it, you give your relationship the gift of authenticity and depth.

Think of vulnerability as a bridge between two people, a way to understand each other on a deeper level. While it can feel uncomfortable, the rewards are immense: trust, intimacy, and the reassurance that you are loved for who you are.

You have the power to be vulnerable, and your relationship can grow stronger. With each step into vulnerability, you and your partner create a more open, honest, and fulfilling connection.

Personal Reflections:

Communication as a Core Tool

Meditation:

Find a quiet, peaceful place to sit or lie down. Please close your eyes and take a deep breath, holding it for a moment before slowly exhaling. Repeat this process several times, allowing yourself to relax fully with each breath.

Now, focus on communication. Imagine a conversation with your partner—a moment where you both feel completely at ease and genuinely heard. Picture the way their eyes meet yours, their tone calm and understanding. Visualize yourself speaking freely and vulnerably, knowing that your words are being received with care.

Pay attention to how this scenario makes you feel. Is there a sense of relief, trust, or connection? Sit with those emotions, letting them wash over you. Effective communication creates a safe space for both partners to express themselves honestly and without fear.

As you sit with this image, repeat this affirmation: **I am committed to fostering open, honest, and respectful communication in my relationship. Through our words, we build a foundation of trust and understanding.**

Practices in Action:

- **Activity 1: The "Check-In" Conversation**
  Set aside dedicated time to have a check-in conversation with your partner. Use this moment to discuss your feelings about the dynamic. Ask open-ended questions, such as:

  - "How are you feeling about where we are in our dynamic?"

  - "Are there any areas you'd like us to focus on or improve?"

  - "What has been working well for you lately?"

  Actively listen to their responses, giving them your full attention. Avoid interrupting or reacting defensively. Let them feel heard and validated.

  Tip: If any concerns arise, take note and agree to revisit them later if they need further discussion. This ensures the conversation stays constructive and safe for both of you.

- **Activity 2: Clarifying Miscommunication**
  Reflect on a recent conversation or situation where miscommunication may have occurred. Discuss it openly with your partner, focusing on understanding their perspective. Work together to clarify intentions and prevent similar misunderstandings in the future.
  Tip: Use phrases like, *"Can you help me understand what you meant by…?"* to keep the conversation neutral and productive.

Journaling Prompt:

1. How has open communication strengthened my dynamic with my partner? Write about specific moments where effective communication helped resolve an issue or deepen your bond.

2. What areas of communication in our dynamic still need improvement? How can I take steps to address those areas?

3. Reflect on how you feel when genuinely heard and understood. How can you ensure your partner feels the same way in your conversations?

Closing Reflection:

Take a moment to breathe deeply, feeling the impact of this meditation settle in your heart and mind. Communication is not just about words; it's about understanding, listening, and creating a space where both partners feel safe and respected.

Remember that communication is a tool that requires regular practice and refinement. Just as you tune an instrument to create harmony, so must you tune your conversations to foster connection and clarity.

Every word, every question, and every moment of listening builds a more vital bridge between you and your partner. By prioritizing communication, you honor your dynamic and the trust that binds you.

You can communicate with love, empathy, and intention. Embrace it, and watch your relationship grow more robust and fulfilling.

Personal Reflections:

Balancing Power and Care

Meditation:

Settle into a calm, undisturbed space where you feel safe. Close your eyes and focus on your breathing—slowly inhaling and exhaling. Let your body relax, releasing any tension in your shoulders, neck, or chest.

Now, imagine the concept of power as energy flowing between you and your partner. Visualize it as a continuous loop—sometimes flowing more strongly in one direction but always returning to create balance. See this energy not as dominance or submission alone but as a partnership where care and trust underpin the entire exchange.

Picture moments when you have cared for your partner in a way that strengthened your bond. Perhaps it was through words of encouragement, physical touch, or simply being present for them. Imagine them reciprocating this care, creating a cycle of love and trust that nourishes both of you.

As you hold this visualization, repeat the affirmation:
Power and care are two sides of the same coin. Our dynamic thrives when we honor both with love and respect.

Practices in Action:

- **Activity 1: Creating a Care Ritual**
  Design a small, meaningful ritual that reinforces mutual care. This could include:

  - A post-scene cuddle where you reconnect emotionally and physically.

  - Exchanging affirmations, like *"Thank you for trusting me"* or *"I appreciate the care you show me."*

  - Preparing a comforting gesture, such as making your partner a favorite drink or meal after an intense moment in your dynamic.

  Tip: Keep the ritual simple but consistent. Rituals act as grounding tools, reminding both partners of the love and care at the heart of your relationship.

- **Activity 2: Identifying Care Needs**
  Sit down with your partner and discuss what care means to you. Ask questions like:

  - "What makes you feel cared for in our dynamic?"

  - "Are there ways I can show care more effectively?"
    Use this opportunity to align your efforts with their needs and vice versa.

Tip: Remember that care can look different for each person—some may value physical affection, while others may prioritize verbal reassurance or acts of service.

Journaling Prompt:

1. How does care manifest in my dynamic with my partner? Reflect on specific actions or moments where care has been given or received.

2. What are the unique ways I show care to my partner, and how do they respond?

3. How can I better balance power and care in our relationship? Are there areas where one feels more dominant than the other?

Closing Reflection:

Take a deep breath and allow yourself to feel gratitude for the role care plays in your dynamic. It is easy to think of power exchange as one-sided, but the truth is that both partners thrive when care is mutual and intentional.

Balancing power and care creates a dynamic that is both empowering and nurturing. It allows each person to feel seen, valued, and supported.

By holding space for care within the framework of power exchange, you honor the humanity in yourself and your partner. Let this balance become a cornerstone of your relationship, ensuring that trust and love flow freely between you.

Remember, power exchange is not just about control—it is about connection. And through care, you strengthen that connection every single day.

Personal Reflections:

Consent as a Living Agreement

Meditation:

Find a quiet space where you can relax fully. Sit comfortably, close your eyes, and take a few deep breaths, allowing your mind and body to settle.

Imagine consent as a living plant—a delicate yet resilient entity that requires constant care. Visualize yourself nurturing this plant. What do you give it? Water for clarity, sunlight for transparency, and fertile soil for trust. As the plant grows, its roots deepen into the foundation of your dynamic, providing stability.

Notice how the plant responds to your attention. When neglected, it may wither; when overbearing control is applied, it may become stunted. But with balance, it thrives, flowering beautifully.

This image reminds you that consent is not a one-time agreement but a living process. It requires regular attention, honest communication, and mutual effort. Repeat the affirmation:
Consent is the cornerstone of our connection. I nurture it with care, respect, and love.

Practices in Action:

- **Activity 1: Creative Consent Roleplay**
  With your partner, engage in a roleplay exercise where you practice asking for consent in unique or playful ways. For example:

    o "May I tie you up with silken threads of passion?"

    o "Would you let me guide you on a journey into your desires tonight?" Experiment with lighthearted, romantic, or poetic language to make consent an engaging and intentional dialogue.

  Tip: Focus on the joy of giving and receiving explicit, enthusiastic consent. Celebrate it as a shared moment of trust and excitement.

- **Activity 2: Consent Check-In Ritual**
  Schedule a regular time—weekly, monthly, or after significant scenes—to sit down with your partner and discuss your boundaries, needs, and desires. Ask questions like:

    o "Are there any boundaries you feel we should revisit?"

    o "Have any of your desires changed or evolved recently?"

    o "How can I make you feel safer and more comfortable in our dynamic?"

Tip: Make this ritual a safe and judgment-free space for both partners to express themselves honestly.

Journaling Prompt:

1. How has my understanding of consent evolved since the beginning of this relationship?

2. In what ways do I actively nurture consent in my dynamic? Are there areas where I could improve?

3. How do I ensure that consent remains an ongoing, living agreement rather than a static understanding?

Closing Reflection:

Consent is the foundation upon which all healthy dynamics are built. It is neither a simple yes or no nor a one-time conversation. Instead, it is a continuous, evolving dialogue that reflects both partners' changing needs, boundaries, and desires.

Treating consent as a living agreement creates a dynamic rooted in respect, care, and mutual understanding. This ongoing process deepens trust and ensures both partners feel valued and safe.

As you move forward, let the image of the thriving plant remind you of the importance of tending to consent with love and intention. When nurtured, it blooms into a beautiful expression of partnership, connection, and shared growth.

Consent is not a limitation but the ultimate expression of respect and care. By honoring it, you strengthen the bond between you and your partner, paving the way for a dynamic filled with trust, joy, and mutual fulfillment.

Personal Reflections:

Exploring Boundaries

Meditation:

Sit in a quiet, comfortable space and close your eyes. Take a few deep breaths, letting your body relax, and your mind settle. Begin to focus on the word **"no."**

Visualize it as a robust and protective shield—not a wall that blocks connection but a barrier that creates safety and trust. This shield makes you feel secure, knowing your boundaries are respected. Notice how it feels to hold this shield firmly yet gently, allowing room for protection and openness.

Now, imagine your partner holding their shield of "no." See how their shield complements yours, forming a mutual space of understanding and respect. Together, these shields don't push you apart; they provide the structure within which trust and intimacy can grow.

Reflect on the power of "no" in your relationship. It is not rejection but an act of self-care and honesty. It builds the foundation for authentic connection, making you feel safe to say **"yes"** wholeheartedly when the moment is right.

Repeat the affirmation:
My boundaries are a source of strength and trust. I honor my "no" and respect my partner's "no" as acts of love and care.

Practices in Action:

- **Activity 1: Create a Boundary Map**
  Sit down with your partner and draw a "boundary map" together. Use concentric circles or layers to represent different comfort levels, from "absolutely yes" in the center to "hard no" on the outermost edge.

  Each partner can list specific activities, words, or scenarios in these layers, visually representing their limits and desires. For example:

  - The inner circle might include things like cuddling or specific roleplay scenarios.

  - The outer circle might include rigid boundaries like certain types of pain or language.

  Tip: Keep this map a living document to revisit and update as your dynamic evolves.

- **Activity 2: Roleplay Boundary Setting**
  Practice saying "no" in a way that feels empowering and respectful. For example, role-play scenarios in which one partner asks for something, and the other practices responding with clear boundaries.

  Example responses:

    - "No, I'm uncomfortable with that right now, but thank you for asking."

    - "I'm not sure about that yet; let's talk more about how it would work for us."

  Tip: This exercise helps normalize boundary setting and reinforces that saying "no" is an act of love, not rejection.

Journaling Prompt:

1. Reflect on a time when you enforced a boundary. How did it feel to stand firm in your needs?

2. What do your boundaries say about your values, desires, and self-respect?

3. How does respecting your partner's boundaries enhance your dynamic?

Closing Reflection:

Boundaries are not barriers to connection; they are the frameworks that allow it to flourish. Saying "no" is not about withholding but about creating a safe space where trust and authenticity thrive.

Boundaries provide clarity and stability in your dynamic. They ensure that both partners can confidently explore their desires and limits, knowing that their needs will be respected. Honoring these limits deepens your bond and creates a foundation for love, growth, and shared exploration.

Remember, boundaries are not static; they evolve as your relationship grows. Revisiting them regularly reinforces your commitment to mutual care and trust. As you move forward, let the strength of your boundaries guide you toward a more fulfilling, connected dynamic.

Boundaries are not walls; they open doors to deeper understanding and intimacy. Honor them, respect them, and let them guide you.

Personal Reflections:

The Role of Patience

Meditation:

Find a quiet space where you can sit comfortably. Close your eyes and take a deep breath, inhaling slowly through your nose and exhaling gently through your mouth. Let your breathing steady and your mind calm as you sink into a state of relaxation.

Now, reflect on the concept of patience in your dynamic. Imagine patience as a soft, steady flame burning brightly within you. It isn't rushed or hurried—it simply exists, offering warmth and light at its own pace.

Picture a moment in your relationship where patience was key—waiting for your partner to open up, adapting to their pace in a scene, or building trust over time. Notice how patience transformed that moment into something meaningful.

With each breath, feel yourself connecting more deeply to this inner flame. Let it remind you that great things—like love, trust, and growth—often require time.

Repeat the affirmation:
Patience strengthens my bond with my partner. I honor the time it takes to nurture our dynamic and embrace the journey, not just the destination.

Practices in Action:

- **Activity 1: Set a Long-Term Goal Together**
  Sit down with your partner and plan a goal that requires time and mutual effort. This could be something specific to your dynamic, such as mastering a new skill, planning a dream scene, or deepening your communication.

  Break the goal into smaller, manageable steps and celebrate each milestone. **Tip:** Use this exercise to practice patience as you work together toward a shared vision.

- **Activity 2: Practice Delayed Gratification**
  Choose an activity or desire within your dynamic and intentionally delay its fulfillment. For example, you could plan an intricate scene and agree to wait a week to experience it.

  During the waiting period, focus on anticipation and preparation. Discuss how this builds excitement and strengthens your connection. **Tip:** Use this time to communicate about expectations, ensuring the eventual experience is even more fulfilling.

Journaling Prompt:

1. Reflect on a time when you showed patience with your partner. What did you learn about yourself and your dynamic in that moment?

2. How has your partner demonstrated patience with you? How did it make you feel?

3. In what areas of your relationship could you practice more patience, and how might this deepen your connection?

Closing Reflection:

Patience is not passive—it is an active choice to nurture and grow your dynamic over time. The steady hand guides your relationship through moments of uncertainty, change, and growth.

Patience allows you to honor each step of your BDSM journey, from building trust to exploring new facets of your connection. It reminds you that the most profound experiences often require time, effort, and care to cultivate.

By embracing patience, you give your dynamic room to flourish. It fosters deeper trust, more transparent communication, and a profound appreciation for your partner and shared journey.

Remember: Patience is the art of waiting with love, intention, and trust. Let it be the flame that lights your path forward.

Personal Reflections:

Strength in Surrender

Meditation:

Find a calm, quiet space where you can reflect undisturbed. Close your eyes and take a deep, slow breath, allowing yourself to relax more deeply with each exhale.

Imagine a moment in which your submissive partner surrenders completely to your care. Visualize their trust as a radiant light that flows between you, glowing brightly in your shared space. Allow this light to remind you of the power in their submission and the depth of their trust in you as their Dominant.

Now, reflect on the responsibility that comes with holding this trust. The act of surrender is not a weakness but a profound strength. It requires vulnerability, but it also reveals the deep connection that exists between you.

Feel the strength in this dynamic—not just your partner's surrender but your ability to guide, protect, and nurture that surrender. Allow this thought to fill you with confidence. As a Dominant, your role is one of leadership and responsibility. Surrender is not about control for control's sake; it's about guiding your partner to explore their limits and desires in a safe, consensual, and loving environment.

With each breath, acknowledge that your leadership is not about domination for domination's sake—it is about providing the space for your partner to feel secure enough to explore their vulnerability with you. Honor the strength in both of you.

Repeat the affirmation:
I honor and protect the trust placed in me. I guide with care and empower with love.

Practices in Action:

- **Activity 1: Guided Relaxation for Connection**
  Lead your partner through a guided relaxation session, either verbally or through touch. Begin by helping them release physical tension, moving from head to toe, and encouraging them to let go of any stress or anxiety. Focus on their breath, helping them settle into the moment. Speak slowly and soothingly, offering affirmations of safety and love as they relax into your control.

  This exercise reinforces the dynamic of trust and surrender, where you, as the Dominant, are the steady force that provides calm and structure. Pay close attention to how they respond—whether through relaxation, deepening breath, or physical cues. Each of these signals their surrender, which you honor with tenderness and patience.

  Tip: Use the pace and tone of your voice to reinforce the control you hold. Ensure they can rely on you for safety and direction during the experience.

- **Activity 2: Symbol of Trust**
  Create or choose a small ritual object that symbolizes your relationship and your partner's trust. It could be something simple, like a small token, a piece of jewelry, or an object that holds personal significance. In your next scene, allow this item to become a visual or physical reminder of your connection.

  As you accept this object, reflect on the strength it represents. It symbolizes submission and demonstrates your responsibility and care as the Dominant. It is a tangible representation of the dynamic you've built together—where both parties give, receive, trust, and guide.

  Tip: Keep this item in a place of reverence—somewhere that reminds both of you of the mutual respect, love, and responsibility you hold. Reflect on the emotional bond it represents and the growth within your dynamic each time it is used.

- **Activity 3: Reinforce the Power of Surrender**
  After a scene or profound moment of surrender, take time to reflect on the experience. Engage with your partner about how they felt during the surrender. Were they able to fully embrace it? Did they feel empowered by letting go, or were there moments of discomfort that you can address together?

  Tip: Be open to feedback and adjust your guidance as needed. Acknowledge that surrender can look different for different individuals and is an evolving process. Your willingness to learn from the experience shows that your leadership is not rigid—it is adaptable and deeply responsive to your partner's needs.

Journaling Prompt:

1. **How do I feel when my partner surrenders to me?** Reflect on your emotional response. Is it a feeling of power, peace, or connection? How do you experience the balance between leading and allowing your partner to be vulnerable?

2. **What emotions arise when I am trusted with their vulnerability?** Consider the deeper layers of responsibility and care you hold in this dynamic. How does this responsibility shape your role as a Dominant?

3. **How can I continue earning my partner's trust?** Reflect on areas where you can deepen your guidance, show more care, or provide additional support. What small rituals or affirmations can strengthen the faith in your dynamic?

4. **How do I ensure that surrender is a safe and empowering experience for my partner?** What steps can you take to create an even more supportive environment in which your partner feels confident surrendering to you?

Closing Reflection:

As a Dominant, your role is not simply to control but to lead with compassion, care, and respect. Your partner's surrender is a sign of the trust they have placed in you. It is not an act of submission to weakness but one of strength and mutual understanding.

Acknowledging the power in their vulnerability, you reaffirm your commitment to protecting and nurturing the dynamic. The balance of power between you and your partner is a dance—sometimes leading, sometimes surrendering, but always trusting and supporting one another.

When you guide with love and responsibility, you empower your partner to surrender fully, creating an environment where you can grow and explore together. The strength in surrender is not just in the act itself but in the bond it forges between you, deepening your connection and reinforcing your trust.

Remember: Your leadership is the key to allowing your partner to explore and embrace their deepest vulnerabilities. By holding that trust with care, you build a dynamic based on respect, love, and the empowering strength of surrender.

Personal Reflections:

Respecting the Power Exchange

Meditation:

Find a quiet, peaceful space where you can focus inward. Close your eyes and take several slow, deep breaths. With each exhale, let go of any tension and allow your body and mind to be calm.

Now, reflect on the power exchange in your dynamic. Picture power as a precious gift—a rare and valuable treasure shared between you and your partner. It cannot be taken lightly or abused but should be nurtured, honored, and respected.

Visualize the flow of power between you. See it not as an imbalance but as a shared energy to which both of you contribute. While the exchange may be unequal sometimes, it is always grounded in mutual consent, understanding, and respect. The power you hold as a Dominant is not a weapon; it is a responsibility that you carry with care and consideration.

Reflect on how you honor that power. Is it with gratitude, humility, and awareness? Does it drive you to be a better leader, a more attentive partner, and a more compassionate guide? Allow yourself to feel the deep reverence that comes with holding this power. Know that proper respect for the exchange means you never take it for granted.

Repeat the affirmation:
I honor the power I hold in this dynamic. I lead with respect, gratitude, and care for the trust placed in me.

Practices in Action:

- **Activity 1: Exchange Letters of Gratitude**
  Take a moment to write a letter of gratitude to your partner. In this letter, express your appreciation for their trust, vulnerability, and the power exchange you share. Acknowledge their strength and courage in surrendering to you, and thank them for the opportunity to lead.

  After writing your letter, exchange it with your partner. Take time to read and reflect on their letter as well. This exchange is not only a way to express your appreciation but also a way to remind each other of the sacredness of the power you share.

  Tip: Make this practice a regular part of your dynamic. Gratitude helps keep the power exchange grounded and ensures both partners feel valued and respected.

- **Activity 2: Reflect on the Responsibility of Power**
  Spend time reflecting on the weight of the responsibility of being a Dominant. Write down your role in the power exchange and how you can continue to honor your partner's trust.

This exercise reminds us that power is not about control for control's sake—it is about service, leadership, and care. The more you reflect on the responsibility that power entails, the more thoughtful and respectful your leadership will become.

Tip: As a Dominant, taking the time to reflect on the responsibility of power shows a deep commitment to your partner's well-being and the success of your dynamic. This reflection strengthens your role as a compassionate leader.

- **Activity 3: Acknowledge Each Other's Roles**
  Take time to acknowledge and appreciate each other's roles within the dynamic. Spend time discussing how both the Dominant and submissive contribute to the power exchange. What strengths do you each bring to the table? How does the submissive's surrender empower you as the Dominant, and how does your guidance empower them?

  This conversation should focus on appreciating and respecting each other's unique contributions. It's easy to get caught up in the act of power play, but it's crucial to remember the mutual respect that is the foundation of any healthy BDSM dynamic.

  Tip: Approach this conversation with openness and an open heart. Be willing to listen and learn how to honor each other's roles better.

Journaling Prompt:

1. **How do I honor the power I hold in this relationship?** Reflect on your actions, words, and attitudes as a Dominant. How do you ensure your energy is used with respect, care, and responsibility?

2. **What does respect look like in this dynamic?** Write about specific actions or words that show respect between you and your partner. How do these actions help reinforce trust, love, and mutual care?

3. **How can I continue to deepen my respect for my partner's role?** Reflect on ways you can show more appreciation for your partner's submission. What small changes or practices could further strengthen your respect for their role in the dynamic?

4. **How do I maintain balance in the power exchange?** Write about how you ensure that your power is used to enhance, not diminish, the connection between you and your partner. How do you avoid taking your power for granted?

Closing Reflection:

The power exchange between you and your partner is not just an agreement; it is a living, breathing entity that must be nurtured and respected. Power is a precious gift, and as the Dominant, it is your responsibility to handle it carefully. The respect you show for your partner's role enhances your bond and strengthens your trust.

Remember that genuine respect means honoring your power, recognizing the dynamic's sacredness, and never taking it for granted. By continuously reflecting on the responsibility that comes with your power, you ensure that you and your partner remain grounded in mutual care, trust, and respect.

The more you honor your role, the more the power exchange will deepen, creating an empowering and nurturing dynamic for both of you. When wielded with respect, power establishes a relationship built on strength, trust, and mutual admiration.

Remember: Your power is a gift—use it wisely, with gratitude, and always in the spirit of mutual respect.

Personal Reflections:

The Importance of Aftercare

Meditation:

Find a comfortable, quiet space to settle into. Please close your eyes and take a slow, deep breath, holding it for a moment before gently releasing it. With each exhale, let go of any tension or stress in your body, allowing yourself to relax fully.

Now, reflect on the emotional impact of aftercare in your dynamic. Aftercare is not just about tending to physical needs—it's about nurturing both partners' emotional and psychological well-being. As the Dominant, think about your responsibility in this experience phase. How do you ensure your partner feels safe, supported, and loved after a scene?

Visualize the comforting, healing aspects of aftercare. Picture yourself gently tending to your partner's emotional state, offering reassurance, affection, and care. Imagine the vulnerability often present after intense scenes and how your presence can bring comfort and grounding.

Affirmation:
I am deeply committed to providing aftercare, ensuring my partner feels emotionally safe, loved, and cared for after every scene. I recognize the power of this moment to deepen our connection and strengthen our trust.

Practices in Action:

- **Activity 1: Create a Post-Scene Aftercare Kit Together**
  Aftercare is a profoundly personal experience, and it's essential to have the right tools at your disposal. Spend time with your partner to create a post-scene aftercare kit. This kit can include items like soothing lotions, blankets, favorite snacks, water, or even personal letters.

  Consider what helps your partner feel comforted and nurtured after a scene. Discuss what kinds of physical and emotional support they might need. Do they prefer silence and stillness, or do they like to talk and share their feelings immediately afterward? Build the kit together, ensuring it caters to your needs and includes the essentials for grounding and comfort.

  Tip: Having an aftercare kit readily available ensures that both partners are prepared for the emotional and physical needs that arise after a scene, helping to provide a sense of security and care.

- **Activity 2: Establish a Post-Scene Routine**
  Develop a post-scene routine with your partner. Aftercare doesn't always have to be complex—it can be a simple and consistent ritual. For example, you might take a moment to cuddle, engage in tender conversation, or offer physical care like wiping away sweat or applying lotion.

This routine should be reassuring and healing for both of you. Discuss with your partner what they need during this time and how you can help them feel grounded and emotionally secure.

Tip: Consistency in aftercare routines helps build a sense of safety and security in your dynamic, allowing both partners to feel confident that their emotional needs will be attended to after each scene.

- **Activity 3: Be Present During Aftercare**
  Aftercare is not just about the items you provide but also about your presence as the Dominant. Reflect on how you can be fully present for your partner during this time. Offer gentle touch, reassurance, and emotional support.

  Make it clear that aftercare is not an afterthought—it's a crucial part of the scene that nurtures the bond between you and your partner. If your partner needs space, respect that, but always ensure they know you are available for comfort and connection.

  Tip: Being present during aftercare shows your partner that your emotional well-being is just as important to you as the physical aspect of the scene.

Journaling Prompt:

1. **What does aftercare look like in our dynamic?** Write about the aftercare practices that resonate most with you and your partner. How does the emotional connection you share deepen during this time?

2. **How can I improve my approach to aftercare?** Reflect on areas where you can enhance your aftercare practices. What actions or words can you offer to help your partner feel more emotionally supported and connected after a scene?

3. **What impact has aftercare had on our relationship?** Write about how aftercare has deepened your emotional connection and strengthened the trust between you and your partner. What benefits have you both noticed in the aftermath of each scene?

4. **How do I respond to my partner's emotional state during aftercare?** Consider how you tune into your partner's emotional needs after a scene. Do you instinctively know how to comfort them, or do you need to check in actively? Reflect on ways to be more mindful and attuned to your partner's emotional state.

Closing Reflection:

Aftercare is not just a routine; it is an essential part of the dynamic that nurtures trust, emotional connection, and intimacy. As a Dominant, your role in aftercare is just as important as your role in the scene itself. Providing comfort, reassurance, and emotional support helps reinforce the bond between you and your partner, ensuring that the experience leaves both of you feeling respected, cared for, and safe.

Remember, aftercare is about more than physical comfort—it is about creating a safe, nurturing space where both partners can come together, reflect, and emotionally support each other. By approaching aftercare with tenderness, compassion, and presence, you strengthen your dynamic's foundation of trust and respect.

The aftercare you provide reflects your commitment to your partner's well-being. It deepens your connection and affirms that the emotional and psychological aspects of the power exchange are just as important as the physical ones.

Remember: Aftercare is a gift, a chance to nurture the emotional bond between you and your partner and ensure that both of you feel safe, supported, and valued.

Personal Reflections:

Embracing Self-Awareness

Meditation:

Find a quiet, comfortable place to sit and take a deep breath. Slowly exhale, allowing your body to relax with each breath. Feel your body's weight grounded in the present moment, letting go of any lingering tension or stress.

As you breathe deeply, turn your attention inward. Focus on your emotions—what are you feeling right now? Whether you are still processing the scene or reflecting on your dynamic, take a moment to observe your feelings without judgment. Are you feeling proud, powerful, tender, or perhaps even conflicted?

As the Dominant, you are responsible for being aware of your emotional state. By acknowledging what you are feeling in this moment, you gain deeper insight into how those emotions influence your actions, decisions, and connection with your partner.

Imagine these emotions as a river—sometimes flowing easily, other times encountering resistance. But no matter the current, you are a steady observer, fully aware of your feelings and how they affect the dynamic. Trust that self-awareness helps you navigate the power exchange with clarity, balance, and respect.

Affirmation:
I embrace my emotions with openness and understanding. I recognize how my emotional state influences the dynamic, and I use my self-awareness to guide my actions and deepen the trust in our relationship.

Practices in Action:

- **Activity 1: Journaling Your Thoughts After a Scene**
  After every scene, spend five minutes journaling your thoughts and emotions. Take note of what you felt during the scene—how did your actions affect the energy between you and your partner? How do you think now that the scene has ended?

  Are there any lingering thoughts, challenges, or joys that arise in this reflection? Journaling your thoughts right after a scene can help you gain clarity and insight into your dynamic's emotional landscape.

  Tip: Don't rush the process. Allow yourself to reflect without expectation or judgment. The goal is not to critique yourself but to understand how you felt and how that experience shapes your role in the relationship.

- **Activity 2: Emotional Check-In with Yourself**
  Set aside time regularly to check in with your emotions. You can do this before or after a scene or during a quiet moment in your daily life. Ask yourself how you're genuinely feeling—beyond surface emotions. Are there any unmet needs, unresolved tensions, or deeper desires you have that need attention?

  Understanding your emotions better equips you to communicate them to your partner and adjust your approach within the dynamic. Self-awareness is a powerful tool for staying present and responsive in the relationship.

  Tip: Write down your thoughts without censoring yourself. This practice helps you identify patterns in your emotional responses and clarifies how to address them with your partner.

- **Activity 3: Share Your Emotional State with Your Partner**
  As you become more aware of your emotions, practice sharing them openly with your partner. This doesn't mean overburdening them with every emotion but communicating your feelings in the moment. Honest emotional sharing fosters deeper connection and understanding, whether it's a post-scene reflection or a regular check-in.

  Tip: Use "I" statements when expressing yourself. For example, "I feel proud of the way the scene went" or "I feel some tension in myself that I need to process." This creates a space for vulnerability and openness, strengthening the dynamic.

Journaling Prompt:

1. **What emotions do I tend to feel most strongly during or after a scene?** Write about how you typically feel during or immediately after a scene. Do you feel more dominant, consequential, or tender? Are there other emotions that arise that may need more attention?

2. **How has my self-awareness impacted my role as a Dominant?** Reflect on how understanding your emotions has shaped your ability to navigate power exchanges. How does your emotional awareness help guide your actions, decisions, and communication?

3. **When have I felt disconnected from my emotions in the dynamic?** Write about a time when you felt emotionally distant or unclear about your feelings. How did it affect your relationship? What steps can you take to reconnect with your emotional state and bring more clarity into the dynamic?

4. **How do I communicate my emotions to my partner healthily?** Reflect on how you share your feelings with your partner. Are there areas where you can improve in expressing your feelings honestly and openly?

Closing Reflection:

Self-awareness is an essential tool in the Dominant's role. It allows you to stay grounded, intentional, and responsive to your dynamic's ever-changing emotional landscape. Understanding and embracing your feelings can create a more balanced, honest, and fulfilling relationship with your partner.

Remember, self-awareness is not just about recognizing your emotions in moments of clarity—it's about understanding how those emotions impact your behavior and the dynamic you share. Embrace this awareness as a powerful tool for growth, deepening trust, and improving communication in your relationship.

The more you understand yourself, the better you can navigate the complexities of power exchange with wisdom, care, and respect. Embrace your feelings, honor them, and use that self-knowledge to build a stronger, more authentic connection with your partner.

Remember: The journey of self-awareness is ongoing. Stay present, stay reflective, and allow yourself the space to grow emotionally as an individual and a Dominant.

Personal Reflections:

Exploring Pleasure in New Ways

Meditation:

Find a comfortable and quiet space to center yourself. Please take a deep breath, hold it for a moment, and then release it slowly. Allow your body to relax with each breath, feeling any tension dissolve.

Now, bring your attention to the idea of exploring pleasure—both yours and your partner's. Picture the two of you discovering something new together, an unfamiliar yet exciting experience. What emotions arise as you think about this? Do you feel curiosity, anticipation, or perhaps a hint of nervousness?

As a Dominant, the power to guide your partner into new experiences is both a privilege and a responsibility. Visualize guiding your partner with care and intention, introducing them to new forms of pleasure while respecting their boundaries. Consider how exploring pleasure can deepen your connection and trust. You are not simply in control of the experience but also present with your partner, sharing in the joy of discovery.

Affirmation:
I embrace the opportunity to explore new pleasures with my partner. I honor their boundaries, carefully guide them, and enjoy our shared experiences. We create new and exciting ways to connect and deepen our bond.

Practices in Action:

- **Activity 1: Trying Something New Together**
  Choose a new activity or experience for you and your partner. This could be a new scene, a different form of play, or exploring a new aspect of your dynamic. Before starting, discuss boundaries, expectations, and any concerns you or your partner may have. Ensure that consent is at the forefront of the conversation.

  Once you have both agreed on the activity, proceed with an open mind, ready to embrace the new experience. Afterward, they checked in with each other to see how the activity felt. Was it pleasurable, challenging, or perhaps somewhere in between? This exploration can become an exciting opportunity for growth in your dynamic.

  Tip: Keep an open mind and be patient. Trying new things takes trust, and it's essential to approach the experience with a sense of curiosity rather than expectation.

- **Activity 2: Setting Boundaries and Expectations**
  Before engaging in a new activity, create clear boundaries and expectations with your partner. Discuss what feels exciting and what may be uncomfortable. It's important to share these thoughts openly, creating a space where both of you feel safe and understood.

You can create a physical or verbal checklist to guide your exploration. This helps ensure that each of you feels heard and respected and provides a framework for clear communication during the activity. If at any point something feels off, you can pause and reassess together.

Tip: Setting expectations beforehand helps prevent misunderstandings and promotes a positive experience. Trust in the exploration process, knowing it's about you experiencing something new together.

- **Activity 3: Sharing Reflection After the Experience**
  After trying the new activity, reflect on the experience with your partner. How did it feel for you both? What worked well, and what could be explored further? This is a time for open, honest communication about what you enjoyed and what might need adjustment.

This reflective practice strengthens communication and builds trust. It reinforces the importance of feedback within the dynamic, ensuring both partners can authentically express themselves and feel heard.

Tip: Approach the reflection with an attitude of curiosity rather than judgment. The goal is to learn and grow together, finding new ways to connect that feel right for both of you.

Journaling Prompt:

1. **What new experiences am I curious about exploring with my partner?** Reflect on any activities or ideas that excite you but may feel out of your comfort zone. Why are you interested in trying these new things? How do they fit within the framework of your dynamic?

2. **How do I feel when introducing new forms of pleasure to my partner?** Write about how you feel in the role of the Dominant as you guide your partner through something unfamiliar. Does it feel empowering, exciting, or even vulnerable at times?

3. **What has been my most rewarding experience exploring new pleasures with my partner?** Reflect on a moment when you and your partner tried something new together. How did it impact your connection? What made the experience meaningful?

4. **How do I ensure my partner feels safe and respected during new experiences?** Write about the steps you take to create a space of safety and consent when trying new activities. How do you communicate your partner's needs and check in with them during the experience?

Closing Reflection:

Exploring new pleasures together is an intimate journey that can deepen your bond, enhance trust, and create more fulfilling experiences in your dynamic. As a Dominant, you have the power to guide your partner and ensure that their comfort, consent, and boundaries are respected.

This exploration is not only about discovering new physical pleasures but also about emotional and psychological growth. The more you share and explore with your partner, the stronger your connection can become. You create a space where both of you feel empowered to step outside your comfort zones and discover new aspects of your dynamic.

Remember, pleasure is not just about the act itself but the shared experience, the trust, and the communication that goes along with it. As you continue to explore together, you'll uncover new layers of connection, intimacy, and trust. The key is approaching it with care, mutual respect, and an open heart.

Embrace the journey of exploration together, knowing that with every new experience, you are creating more profound, meaningful connections with your partner.

Personal Reflections:

Honoring Limits

Meditation:

Find a quiet space where you can focus without distraction. Close your eyes and take a deep breath in, holding it for a moment and slowly releasing the air. Let your body relax with each breath.

Imagine a line in the sand—a boundary, a limit you've drawn for yourself and your partner. This line represents what you are not willing to cross, the boundaries that define your comfort and safety. Feel the strength and firmness of this line as it stands in place, protecting you both.

As a Dominant, you have a responsibility to recognize, respect, and honor these limits, both your own and your partner's. This boundary isn't just a line; it's a marker of respect, a promise that the dynamic will be one of care, safety, and understanding. The power you hold within the relationship includes the ability to enforce these boundaries with care and clarity.

Reflect on what protects these limits. Is it trust, mutual respect, or open communication? Whatever it may be, acknowledge the importance of these protections as you move forward. You are ensuring that the experience is safe and remains positive and fulfilling for both of you.

Affirmation:
I honor the limits that I have set and the ones my partner shares with me. I protect these boundaries with care, understanding, and respect. My limits define my self-respect and safety, empowering our dynamic to grow stronger with trust.

Practices in Action:

- **Activity 1: Discussing Limits Openly**
  Have an open conversation with your partner about your hard and soft limits. Discuss what each of you feels comfortable with and what may be off-limits. Understanding the nuances of each other's boundaries allows you to respect them more fully and prevent misunderstandings.

  Hard limits are those non-negotiable boundaries—activities or behaviors you are unwilling to engage in. Soft limits, on the other hand, are areas where you might be open to exploring but require care, negotiation, or gradual trust-building. Having this conversation allows both of you to feel heard and respected.

  Tip: Keep the conversation ongoing. Limits can evolve as trust deepens, but they should always be respected.

- **Activity 2: Creating a Boundary Map**
  Sit down with your partner and create a visual representation of your boundaries. Draw a map of your relationship dynamic, with lines or circles indicating your hard and soft limits. Use this tool to guide your interactions and ensure that both of you are clear on where the boundaries lie.

  By visualizing your limits, you create a tangible understanding of what is acceptable and what is not. This map reminds us to always check in with each other about boundaries and be conscious of respecting them during scenes or discussions.

  Tip: Don't just create the map once—update it regularly. As you grow and evolve together, so will your understanding of each other's limits.

- **Activity 3: Reaffirming Limits After Each Scene**
  After a scene or an intimate experience, take time to check in with your partner and reaffirm the boundaries that were set. Did anything feel too much, too little, or uncomfortable? This is an opportunity to address emotional or physical reactions to the experience and adjust for future interactions.

  By reaffirming your limits after each experience, you reinforce a mutual understanding of respect and care. This practice ensures both partners feel safe, heard, and respected.

  Tip: Be open to feedback. Understanding how your partner feels after a scene is just as important as how you communicate your limits.

Journaling Prompt:

1. **What are my hard and soft limits, and how do they protect my sense of safety and self-respect?** Reflect on how understanding boundaries helps you control your emotional and physical well-being. How do these limits help shape the dynamic in a safe and empowering way?

2. **How does honoring my partner's limits strengthen our dynamic?** Respecting your partner's boundaries enhances trust, communication, and connection. How does it affect your emotional bond?

3. **What challenges have I faced in respecting my own or my partner's limits?** Reflect on a time when a limit was tested or pushed. What was the outcome, and how did you work through it together?

4. **How can I further honor my partner's limits while still being an active and engaged Dominant?** Consider ways to incorporate respect for limits into your leadership role. How can you create a safe, nurturing space while guiding your partner through new experiences?

Closing Reflection:

Honoring limits is essential in any relationship, particularly within a BDSM dynamic. As a Dominant, you hold a certain amount of control, but with that power comes the responsibility to respect the boundaries that protect you and your partner. These limits are safeguards and symbols of trust and mutual respect.

When you honor limits, you build a foundation of safety where both partners feel empowered to explore their desires and grow within the dynamic. Boundaries provide a structure for freedom, creativity, and trust, ensuring each experience remains positive and consensual.

Ultimately, respecting and understanding limits allows for more profound emotional connection, trust, and satisfaction in your relationship. It ensures that both partners can explore, evolve, and enjoy their dynamic within a safe and mutually supportive environment.

Honor the limits that protect your trust and connection, knowing that these boundaries are the pillars that uphold your shared journey of growth and pleasure.

Personal Reflections:

Handling Mistakes with Grace

Meditation:

Find a quiet, comfortable place to sit and close your eyes. Please take a deep, grounding breath, holding it for a moment before slowly releasing it. Feel the weight of any tension or stress leave your body as you exhale. Allow yourself to settle into a peaceful state of mind.

Now, reflect on the concept of mistakes. We are all human, and mistakes are inevitable in any relationship. As a Dominant, you may feel responsible for creating and maintaining the dynamic, but it's essential to recognize that mistakes are not failures but opportunities for growth and understanding.

Visualize a mistake that may have occurred in the past—perhaps a boundary was unintentionally crossed, or communication was misinterpreted. Rather than focusing on the negative feelings that might have emerged, concentrate on the lessons learned and how the experience strengthened your relationship.

Mistakes offer an opportunity to demonstrate grace, patience, and humility. They allow both partners to practice vulnerability, repair any damage done, and rebuild trust. Imagine yourself in this moment of resolution—how do you respond with compassion and care? How do you honor the process of reconciliation and growth?

Affirmation:
I acknowledge that mistakes are a natural part of our journey together. I handle them with grace, patience, and understanding. I use them as opportunities to strengthen our connection and deepen our trust. I am committed to learning and growing with my partner, even in challenging moments.

Practices in Action:

- **Activity 1: Roleplaying Apology and Repair**
  Roleplay is a scenario where a boundary is unintentionally crossed. As the Dominant, practice apologizing and taking responsibility for the misstep. Acknowledge the mistake without defensiveness, demonstrating genuine empathy for your partner's feelings.

  After the apology, discuss how to repair the situation. What steps can you both take to ensure the boundary is respected in the future? How can you rebuild trust and demonstrate that you value your partner's emotional and physical well-being?

  Tip: Sincerity is the key to an effective apology. Acknowledge how your actions impacted your partner and express a genuine desire to do better in the future.

- **Activity 2: Creating a Repair Ritual**
Create a ritual or practice after a mistake has been made. This might include a dedicated conversation to discuss what happened and a symbolic gesture of reconnection. This ritual can be anything from a shared quiet moment together to affirming your commitment to each other.

  This activity aims to foster a sense of safety and healing. Mistakes don't have to be seen as setbacks; instead, they can become moments to reaffirm the strength of your connection and the resilience of your bond.

  Tip: Focus on actions that restore emotional balance. Physical gestures of affection—such as a gentle touch or holding hands—can help reaffirm trust and care.

- **Activity 3: Establishing a Mistake-Resolution Framework**
Have an open conversation with your partner about how you both handle mistakes. What approach works best for each of you when something goes wrong? Do you prefer immediate resolution, or do you need time to process? How can you ensure that mistakes are addressed in a way that promotes learning and healing rather than blame?

  Tip: This conversation should be about creating a safe space where both partners feel heard and supported. The goal is not to place blame but to work collaboratively to resolve the issue and move forward together.

Journaling Prompt:

1. **How do I respond when a mistake is made in the dynamic?** Reflect on past instances where you or your partner made a mistake. How did you handle the situation, and what did you learn from it? Did it lead to growth, or did it feel like a setback?

2. **What does grace look like in these moments of tension?** Write about how you can embrace grace, not just for your partner but for yourself. How can you release guilt or frustration and shift your focus to reconciliation and learning?

3. **How does resolving mistakes strengthen trust in our relationship?** Consider how working through challenges has deepened your bond. What role does vulnerability play in repairing trust, and how does it lead to a stronger, more resilient connection?

4. **What can I do differently to handle mistakes with more compassion and understanding?** Reflect on your responses to errors and how they could be improved. Are there new tools or approaches you can implement to ensure your actions align with the values of empathy, growth, and care?

Closing Reflection:

Mistakes are a natural part of any relationship, especially one that involves power dynamics like BDSM. They are not signs of failure but invitations to grow, heal, and deepen your connection. As a Dominant, your ability to handle mistakes gracefully is a testament to your leadership. By acknowledging your imperfections and working through mistakes with humility and care, you create an environment where both partners feel safe, supported, and loved.

Remember that your relationship is not defined by your mistakes but by how you respond to them. With patience, empathy, and a commitment to growth, you can turn every mistake into an opportunity to strengthen the bond between you and your partner.

By resolving mistakes together, you forge deeper trust, a more resilient connection, and a shared understanding that you are both committed to supporting each other through the ups and downs of your journey.

Mistakes are not the end but the beginning of a stronger, more compassionate relationship. Embrace them with grace and allow your connection to grow even more vital.

Personal Reflections:

Playfulness in the Dynamic

Meditation:

Find a calm, comfortable space to sit and close your eyes. Take a slow, deep breath, filling your lungs with air, and hold it for a moment before gently exhaling. Allow tension or stress to melt away as you focus on your breath, becoming grounded and centered.

Now, envision a moment of shared laughter between you and your partner. Picture the two of you in a lighthearted moment, where the pressure of roles and expectations dissolves, and you can enjoy each other's company. Perhaps you're sharing an inside joke, teasing each other playfully, or being silly together.

Reflect on how playfulness feels in the dynamic. As the Dominant, you may find that these moments of levity create a space for connection free from the weight of responsibility or authority. Playfulness can strip away any pretense, allowing you and your partner to interact as equals, even while maintaining your roles.

Notice how your body feels in this moment of joy. Can you feel the warmth of laughter in your chest? Can you sense the closeness and trust that come with shared fun moments? Let that feeling expand; knowing playfulness is essential to a healthy dynamic.

Affirmation:
I welcome and encourage playfulness in our dynamic. I recognize that laughter and lightheartedness foster trust, intimacy, and connection. I embrace these moments as opportunities to deepen our bond and enjoy the journey together.

Practices in Action:

- **Activity 1: Plan a Lighthearted Scene**
  Set aside time to create a fun, non-serious scene to explore with your partner. This scene doesn't need to follow the traditional intensity of power dynamics; instead, it focuses on humor, role reversals, or playful scenarios. You could dress up in silly outfits, share a playful task (like a "punishment" that's light and humorous), or engage in an activity where laughter is the primary goal.

  The key is to let go of any seriousness and enjoy the moment. This activity can help break down walls and build a sense of camaraderie and connection beyond the roleplay or the scene itself.

  Tip: Embrace spontaneity! Let the scene evolve naturally without overthinking the details. Playfulness thrives in the absence of expectations.

- **Activity 2: Teasing and Playful Power Reversals**
  Playfully tease each other in a way that reinforces your bond. Try gentle role reversals, where the Dominant takes on a more submissive or silly role or where you both engage in an activity that encourages mutual vulnerability without diminishing the power dynamic.

  Playful teasing can lighten the mood, remind you that the dynamic doesn't always need to be severe or intense, and allow you to explore a different kind of intimacy grounded in trust and affection.

  Tip: Keep it light and ensure that both partners are comfortable with the level of playfulness. Consent should always remain at the forefront of these interactions.

- **Activity 3: Laughter as a Bonding Tool**
  Share a moment of laughter in an unplanned, spontaneous way. This might be watching a funny movie together, playing a lighthearted game, or even sharing a funny story. Notice how laughter shifts the energy between you. Does it feel like a release? Does it help you connect in a new way?

  Tip: Keep the mood light and positive. The goal is to enjoy the playful exchange and experience how laughter enhances the connection between you and your partner.

Journaling Prompt:

1. **What moments of laughter stand out in our dynamic?** Write about when you and your partner shared a moment of genuine, carefree joy. How did that affect your connection? How did it influence the power dynamic, if at all?

2. **How does playfulness affect how I view my role in the relationship?** Reflect on how playfulness impacts your relationship with power and control. Does it make you feel more relaxed in your role as the Dominant, or does it reinforce your connection differently?

3. **What role do humor and laughter play in our intimacy?** Consider how humor allows for vulnerability, openness, and connection. Does playfulness help build trust, and if so, how?

4. **How can we incorporate more moments of joy and laughter into our dynamic?** Think about how you can intentionally create space for playfulness. How can you foster more joy in your relationship through shared activities, spontaneous moments, or playful roleplay?

Closing Reflection:

Playfulness is about humor and deepening the emotional connection between you and your partner. As the Dominant, it's easy to focus solely on the intensity and responsibility of the dynamic. Still, moments of laughter and lightheartedness remind both of you that you can be yourself, relaxed and joyful, within the dynamic.

Through shared play, you build intimacy without relying on control or dominance. Instead, it's about trusting each other enough to embrace vulnerability and silliness. This openness creates space for growth and connection, strengthening the relationship in ways that power exchanges alone cannot.

Remember that your dynamic is multifaceted. Just as you honor the serious and profound moments, also honor the playful and light ones. Both are essential in fostering a deeply fulfilling connection rooted in love, trust, and mutual respect.

Playfulness is not just a release but a pathway to deeper intimacy and a more enriched dynamic. Embrace it with an open heart, and let it be a joyful part of your journey together.

Personal Reflections:

Celebrating Small Victories

Meditation:

Take a deep, grounding breath. Close your eyes and focus on your breath—slowly inhaling through your nose and gently exhaling through your mouth. With each breath, let go of any tension or distractions, allowing yourself to be fully present.

Now, reflect on a recent achievement or milestone within your dynamic. It could be something as simple as a thriving scene, clear communication, or even a subtle shift in trust or vulnerability. Please take a moment to truly appreciate this victory, no matter how small it may seem. Acknowledge the effort and intention that went into it, knowing that every step forward, no matter how small, contributes to the overall growth of your dynamic.

Think about how you feel at this moment. Is there a sense of pride, satisfaction, or gratitude? Allow these positive emotions to settle deeply within you. Visualize this achievement as a bright light within you, radiating pride and accomplishment. As a Dominant, your guidance, care, and commitment have shaped this success, and you deserve to honor your role in this growth.

Affirmation:
I celebrate every victory, no matter how small. I acknowledge the growth within myself and my partner. I am proud of our journey and the progress we continue to make together.

Practices in Action:

- **Activity 1: Celebrate with a Small Reward**
  Take a moment to celebrate your growth together. This doesn't need to be a grand gesture—sometimes, small acknowledgments are the most meaningful. Whether it's sharing a thoughtful moment, gifting each other something simple yet significant, or taking time to relax and enjoy each other's company, the goal is to honor the growth that's taken place.

  Tip: This can be a verbal acknowledgment ("I'm proud of us for how we handled that scene today") or a physical gesture like a hug, a favorite treat, or simply sitting together in quiet gratitude. The reward doesn't need to be extravagant; what matters is the shared recognition of progress.

- **Activity 2: Acknowledge and Share Your Progress**
  Sit down with your partner and acknowledge what both of you have achieved. This could be a specific achievement in the dynamic (like successfully exploring a new boundary or navigating a difficult conversation) or broader, like the growth in your connection over time. Express how proud you are of both of you and share any personal milestones or shifts you've noticed in your growth.

Tip: When sharing your pride in each other, focus on the positive and the progress made instead of any "lack" or areas for improvement. This is about reinforcing the growth, not focusing on what's still left to work on.

- **Activity 3: Reflecting on Growth**
  Spend a few minutes reflecting on the growth you've experienced within your dynamic. You can do this through journaling or simply by taking quiet time together to verbalize your thoughts. What moments of growth, both big and small, stand out? How have these victories shaped your connection and your relationship?

  Tip: Use this time to express gratitude for each other. Celebrate the commitment, trust, and effort that go into each step forward, acknowledging how every small victory builds upon the last.

Journaling Prompt:

1. **What recent victory are you most proud of in your dynamic?** Write about the specific achievement that has had the most impact on your journey so far. How did it make you feel to reach this milestone? What did you learn from it?

2. **How has recognizing small victories changed your perspective on your relationship?** Celebrating the little wins has made you feel more connected to your partner. Does it encourage you to keep moving forward with more confidence and positivity?

3. **How can you continue to honor the small victories as you move forward in your dynamic?** Think about ways to keep recognizing and celebrating growth. How can this practice become a regular part of your journey together?

4. **What role does acknowledgment play in strengthening your relationship?** Reflect on how celebrating big or small victories affects your bond. Does it help reinforce trust? Does it allow you to feel more deeply connected to your partner?

Closing Reflection:

Remember that every step forward, no matter how small, is a triumph in your journey together. As the Dominant, it's essential to recognize that the path to growth and deepening connection is filled with small victories. These moments are the building blocks of a more fulfilling dynamic, and celebrating them allows you to honor the effort and dedication you both bring to the relationship.

Celebrating these victories deepens the bond between you and your partner and fosters a sense of achievement and positivity that propels both of you toward further growth. By focusing on progress rather than perfection, you create an environment where both of you can thrive.

Take time to celebrate your victories. Every moment of growth, every victory, no matter how small, is worth honoring.

Personal Reflections:

Understanding Each Other's Needs (Dominant's Perspective)

Meditation:

Find a comfortable, quiet space to center yourself. Close your eyes and take a slow, deep breath, allowing the air to fill your lungs. Hold for a moment, then exhale slowly, releasing tension or distractions. Let each breath bring you deeper into calm, focus, and connection.

Now, turn your attention inward and focus on your partner's emotional and physical needs. Imagine what it might feel like to understand and support them in every way they require. Reflect on how you've responded to these needs and continue to do so, sometimes in ways that might surprise you.

Visualize your connection with your partner as a dance, where you take turns leading and following, always in sync with one another's rhythms and desires. As the Dominant, you may find strength in anticipating and meeting your partner's needs before they ask. Yet, it's just as important to acknowledge that you are constantly learning about these needs, which may change with time, growth, and experience.

Now, take a moment to check in with your own feelings—how do you feel about your partner's needs? Do you feel proud of how you support them? Or perhaps you have a deeper awareness of areas where you can offer even more. Recognizing the importance of this connection will deepen your ability to meet their needs with empathy and confidence.

Affirmation:
I am attuned to my partner's needs and meet them with care and compassion. I recognize that our needs evolve and am committed to understanding and responding to them with respect and love.

Practices in Action:

- **Activity 1: Reflect and Discuss Needs**
  Take time to have an open and honest conversation with your partner about each other's emotional and physical needs. Ask each other: *How have your needs changed over time? What do you need from each other right now?* It's essential to listen with empathy and without judgment. Acknowledge that needs can shift and that it's okay to communicate those changes freely.

  Tip: During this conversation, approach your partner with curiosity and care. This is not about solving problems but about understanding them on a deeper level. Make sure you're giving space for your needs to be expressed fully.

- **Activity 2: Meeting Emotional and Physical Needs**
  Think of a need your partner has expressed recently. What can you do to support them in fulfilling that emotional and physical need? Whether offering words of affirmation, providing comfort, or exploring something new together, focus on finding a way to respond to their needs in a way that makes them feel heard and valued. This may include offering more time together, increasing your presence, or even learning something new that aligns with their desires.

  Tip: Responding to your partner's needs is not always about fulfilling them immediately but showing consistent willingness to engage and understand. Sometimes, just asking, "How can I be there for you right now?" can create the space for genuine connection.

- **Activity 3: Checking in Regularly**
  Make it a habit to regularly check in with each other about your needs, desires, and feelings. This isn't just a one-time conversation—it's an ongoing process of communication that ensures both partners remain aligned. By checking in frequently, you create a safe environment where both partners feel secure enough to share their needs without fear of judgment.

  Tip: This doesn't have to be a formal conversation every time. Small moments of acknowledgment, like asking, *"Is there anything you need from me today?"* can make a big difference in staying connected and understanding each other.

Journaling Prompt:

1. **What needs does my partner have that I feel confident in meeting?** Reflect on the emotional and physical needs of your partner that you can meet. How does it feel to provide this support?

2. **What needs of my partner have I overlooked or struggled with meeting?** Write about any areas where you feel there is room for growth or improvement in understanding or fulfilling your partner's needs. What would it take to address those areas more effectively?

3. **How do my own needs interact with my partner's?** Consider how your needs and your partner's needs balance. Do you feel that both of you can express and meet each other's needs in a way that feels fair and fulfilling? How can this balance be strengthened?

4. **How can I proactively meet my partner's needs?** Reflect on ways you can show more initiative in understanding and fulfilling your partner's emotional and physical needs. Are there new ways you can approach this?

Closing Reflection:

As the dominant in your dynamic, learning about your partner's evolving needs is vital. You may find that by being more attuned to these needs, you strengthen your connection and increase the depth of your care and commitment. Remember that meeting each other's needs is not a one-way street—it's a shared responsibility that brings you closer, fostering trust, respect, and mutual understanding.

Honoring your partner's needs creates a strong foundation for growth and connection, allowing both of you to thrive in your roles. Continually reflecting on how those needs are met ensures that your relationship remains dynamic, healthy, and fulfilling.

Commit to understanding and responding to your partner's needs, knowing that this will deepen your bond and strengthen the foundation of trust and respect in your dynamic.

Personal Reflections:

Building Rituals Together

Meditation:

Find a quiet, peaceful space where you can sit comfortably without distractions. Close your eyes and take a deep, cleansing breath. Inhale slowly, filling your lungs with air, and then exhale slowly, releasing any tension or distractions. Allow yourself to become fully present, focusing on your connection with your partner.

Now, envision a ritual that grounds both of you, symbolizing your bond and reinforcing your roles. This ritual doesn't need to be grand, but it should be meaningful. Perhaps it's a simple act you can perform together, such as a shared word or phrase that marks the beginning or end of your dynamic for the day. Or it could be something physical—a gesture, a touch, a look—that reaffirms your trust and connection.

As you reflect on this ritual, consider its purpose. What does it offer you and your partner? Does it help create a sense of safety, grounding, or connection? How can you deepen its significance over time? With each repetition, you may find that this ritual becomes an essential part of your relationship, bringing both of you closer and strengthening the trust and understanding you share.

Affirmation:
I honor the rituals we build together. They are expressions of our connection, trust, and love. These rituals ground me in my role and deepen my bond with my partner.

Practices in Action:

- **Activity 1: Designing Your Ritual**
  Work together to design a meaningful ritual that reflects your unique dynamic. This could be a ritual you practice before or after a scene or a daily or weekly activity that reminds you both of the roles you hold and the connection you share. Perhaps you both exchange a word of affirmation or gratitude, or you engage in a simple service that subtly and meaningfully honors the Dominant/submissive roles.

  Tip: The best rituals resonate emotionally with both of you, creating a sense of grounding and intimacy. Make sure this ritual feels authentic to your dynamic, and allow it to evolve naturally as your relationship grows.

- **Activity 2: Integrating Rituals Into Daily Life**
  Once you've created a ritual, incorporate it into your daily or weekly routine. This could be as simple as saying a phrase before parting ways each morning or taking a few moments to check in with each other at the end of the day. Alternatively, your ritual could be tied to a specific event in your dynamic—like preparing for a scene together or celebrating a shared achievement.

Tip: Rituals don't have to be complex or time-consuming. Even small acts of connection, when done consistently, can profoundly strengthen your relationship and deepen your roles.

- **Activity 3: Reflecting on the Meaning of the Ritual**
  After you've practiced your ritual a few times, please take a moment to reflect on its impact. How does it make you feel when you engage in it? Does it enhance your connection? Do you find yourself feeling more grounded and in tune with your partner? Use this time to appreciate the significance of what you've created together and to consider how it might evolve or grow as your dynamic deepens.

  Tip: Rituals can evolve as your relationship grows. If something no longer feels aligned with your connection, feel free to adjust or create new rituals that are more reflective of where you are now.

Journaling Prompt:

1. **What ritual would best represent the connection and trust we share?** Consider what kind of ritual feels most meaningful to you and your partner. How can it reflect the essence of your relationship?

2. **How does this ritual deepen our understanding of our roles?** Write about how engaging in this ritual makes you feel like you are in your dominant role. How does it help strengthen the bond between you and your partner, and how does it reaffirm your connection?

3. **What impact does this ritual have on our dynamic?** Reflect on how your ritual influences your relationship. Does it deepen trust, create a sense of security, or enhance intimacy? How does it make both you and your partner feel?

4. **How can we continue to evolve our rituals to reflect our growth?** Rituals are living things that grow with you. How can your ritual evolve as your dynamic deepens or your roles shift?

Closing Reflection:

The rituals you create together are more than just actions—they are expressions of your bond, a reflection of your shared trust, and a testament to the strength of your dynamic. These rituals, no matter how small, offer grounding and connection, helping you both stay present in the moment and focused on the trust you share. They remind you of your roles and the importance of intentionally honoring them.

Building rituals that reflect your values and roles strengthens your connection and creates a deeper sense of security and intimacy. As your dynamic continues to evolve, these rituals will serve as a constant reminder of your commitment to each other, allowing you both to thrive in your roles.

Trusting Your Intuition

Meditation:

Find a quiet space to relax and breathe deeply. Close your eyes and focus on your breath—slowly inhaling through your nose and exhaling through your mouth. Allow your body to relax with each breath, releasing tension or distractions. Let yourself be fully present in this moment.

Now, reflect on a time when your intuition guided you well. Perhaps it was a moment in your dynamic when you felt a subtle pull or a quiet knowing that led you to choose or take an action that brought you closer to your partner. Trusting your gut in that moment likely felt empowering, confirming that your inner wisdom is always available.

Think about how your intuition works in your relationship—how it informs your decisions, guides your actions, and strengthens the connection with your partner. What does it feel like when you follow your intuition? Trust that your inner voice is a vital tool in navigating your dynamic, and recognize that it offers valuable guidance regarding your roles and the power you share.

Affirmation:
I trust my intuition to guide me in my role. It is a powerful tool that strengthens my connection with my partner, ensuring our dynamic remains balanced, safe, and fulfilling. I listen to my inner voice and honor the wisdom it brings.

Practices in Action:

- **Activity 1: Tuning Into Your Intuition**
  In your next scene or intimate moment, take a moment to pause and check in with yourself. Ask, "Does this feel right?" Take a deep breath and notice how your body and mind respond. Are there any feelings of discomfort, hesitation, or excitement? Allow yourself to trust what you sense, and let your intuition guide you toward the best course of action. It may be a shift in energy, a need for more space, or a deeper connection. Whatever it is, trust that your intuition is helping you navigate the dynamic.

  Tip: It can be easy to rush through moments without pausing, but taking a breath and listening to your intuition can deepen your awareness and help you create a more harmonious experience. Practice trusting your instincts and distinguish between your intuition and outside influences.

- **Activity 2: Reflecting on Past Intuitive Moments**
  Take time to reflect on a situation in your dynamic where trusting your intuition led to a positive outcome. Perhaps there was a moment when you sensed your partner's needs before they could express them or when following your instincts allowed you to create a moment of vulnerability or connection. Journaling about this experience can help you tap into that intuitive wisdom again in the future.

Tip: When reflecting on your intuitive moments, notice how they align with your understanding of your role. Your intuition often reflects your subconscious knowledge of your partner's needs and the trust you share, so pay attention to how it guides you.

- **Activity 3: Strengthening Your Intuition**
  Practice mindfulness outside of your dynamic to strengthen your ability to trust your intuition. Engage in activities that help you tune into your body and mind, such as meditation, yoga, or journaling. The more attuned you are to your inner self, the easier it becomes to hear and trust your intuition when needed.

  Tip: Trusting your intuition is a skill that deepens with practice. Be patient with yourself as you cultivate this trust. Over time, your intuitive insights will become clearer and more reliable, especially when it comes to making decisions in your dynamic.

Journaling Prompt:

1. **When have I trusted my intuition in the past, and how did it guide me?** Write about a moment when your intuition led you to decide or take action that positively impacted your dynamic. What was the feeling at that moment, and what was the outcome?

2. **How does my intuition show up in our dynamic?** Reflect on how your intuition guides you as a Dominant. Does it help you sense your partner's needs or inform your decisions about boundaries, trust, or care?

3. **How can I strengthen my intuition and trust it more fully in the future?** Consider practices or activities that could help you sharpen your intuitive abilities. How can you create more space in your daily life to connect with your inner wisdom and use it in your dynamic?

Closing Reflection:

Intuition is a powerful and often underappreciated tool in any relationship. When you trust your instincts, you strengthen your connection with your partner and honor the deep wisdom within you. By pausing to listen to your inner voice, you allow it to guide your decisions, actions, and interactions, ensuring your dynamic remains healthy and authentic.

Trusting your intuition doesn't mean ignoring logic or boundaries. Instead, it's about finding a balance between your gut feelings and the practical aspects of your relationship. Your intuition is a compass—one that, when tuned in to, can guide you through even the most complex moments with ease.

As you continue to nurture your intuition and practice listening to it, you will find that it leads you to more fulfilling, meaningful, and connected experiences within your dynamic. Trust yourself, your partner, and the wisdom that resides within both of you.

Personal Reflections:

The Role of Control and Letting Go

Meditation:

Find a quiet space where you can sit comfortably. Close your eyes and begin to take slow, deep breaths. Inhale deeply through your nose, filling your lungs, and exhale gently through your mouth, letting go of any tension in your body. With each breath, allow yourself to relax further, becoming more present.

Reflect on the delicate balance between holding control and letting go. As a Dominant, you are accustomed to guiding and leading your dynamic, but there are times when letting go of that control can create deeper intimacy and trust. Contemplate how it feels to hold control—how empowering it can be to set boundaries, give direction, and shape the experience. Now, shift your focus and think about the moments when you choose to relinquish control. What does it feel like to let your partner take the lead, even temporarily? How does this act of trust strengthen the bond between you both?

Let yourself acknowledge that letting go of control does not mean losing power; it's a different kind of strength. It is an act of vulnerability that invites your partner to step into their power while still honoring the dynamic you share. Let this realization settle in, trusting that your ability to hold and release control can create a richer, more balanced dynamic.

Affirmation:
I embrace the balance between control and letting go. I trust that relinquishing control, even temporarily, creates space for growth, connection, and mutual respect. My power lies in guiding my partner and knowing when to step back and allow them to lead.

Practices in Action:

- **Activity 1: Roleplaying Letting Go**
  Roleplay a scene where you, as the Dominant, intentionally let go of control and allow your partner to take charge temporarily. This could be something as simple as allowing them to direct the scene or choose the following action. Notice how this shift in power feels—are there moments of discomfort or excitement? Reflect on how the change in dynamics opens up new avenues of connection and trust.

  Tip: Let go to explore, rather than control, the experience. This practice can help build trust and remind both partners of the fluid nature of power in your relationship.

- **Activity 2: Reflection on Power Dynamics**
  After practicing relinquishing control, reflect on how power flows within your dynamic. Write about moments when you have held control and let go. How do you feel in each of these roles? How does the act of allowing affect your relationship and trust?

Tip: If there are moments when relinquishing control feels challenging, consider why that might be. Are there fears or insecurities that arise when you are not in charge? Explore these feelings as an opportunity for growth.

- **Activity 3: Trusting Your Partner's Leadership**
  During your next scene, allow your partner to take charge for some time. This could involve them directing the pace or choosing how the scene unfolds. Practice surrendering your need for control and trusting they will respect the dynamic. Afterward, discuss how it felt to shift the power and what you learned from the experience.

  Tip: Clear communication before and after this exercise is important. Both partners should feel safe and supported throughout the process, and any boundaries or concerns should be addressed beforehand.

Journaling Prompt:

1. **What does it feel like for me to relinquish control of our dynamic?** Reflect on specific moments when you have allowed your partner to take charge. What emotions or thoughts arise? How does it affect the way you perceive your role?

2. **How do I balance holding control and letting go?** Write about the challenges or benefits you experience when navigating this balance. Does it deepen your connection or bring up fear or resistance?

3. **In what areas of our dynamic can I practice letting go of control more?** Reflect on where and why you might most resist relinquishing control. Consider small ways to practice letting go and trusting your partner in those moments.

Closing Reflection:

Control and the ability to let go are essential parts of your role as a Dominant. The strength in relinquishing control comes from trusting that your partner will hold the space safely and respectfully and that your bond is strong enough to allow flexibility and fluidity.

Letting go doesn't diminish your power; it enhances it. It fosters a sense of mutual respect and deepens the emotional intimacy between you and your partner. When you can surrender control, even briefly, you allow for new experiences, growth, and a more profound connection.

Remember, the dance between holding and releasing control is one of the most potent aspects of your dynamic. It reminds you that power is not static but can be shared and exchanged in ways that strengthen your bond.

By embracing the moments when you let go, you create space for trust, vulnerability, and a deeper understanding of each other's roles in your dynamic.

Exploring Desire Through Introspection

Meditation:

Find a comfortable space to sit quietly and focus on your breath. Close your eyes, take a deep breath through your nose, and exhale slowly through your mouth. Let the rhythm of your breath help you center your mind and relax your body.

As you settle into this space, begin to turn your attention inward. Reflect on the sources of your desires—what excites you most and why? Consider what aspects of your dynamic bring you the most satisfaction, and explore the deeper emotions tied to those desires. Is it the control, the trust, the vulnerability, or perhaps the emotional connection that stirs your passion?

As you focus on these desires, allow yourself to explore them without judgment. Let your mind wander freely through different scenarios, sensations, and experiences. Ask yourself: what do you truly desire, and how can you embrace these desires with integrity, respect, and mindfulness? Allow the answers to surface naturally without rushing or forcing them.

Affirmation:
I honor my desires and the journey of exploration they take me on. I embrace the vulnerability that comes with being open about my needs and the trust that allows my desires to unfold healthily and consensually.

Practices in Action:

- **Activity 1: Identifying and Sharing Desires**
  Take time to explore your desires, both sexual and emotional, on a deeper level. Once you've reflected on them, share your deepest desires with your partner. Allow yourself to be open and vulnerable, expressing what excites you the most and why. Share your fantasies and the emotional aspects tied to those desires. This practice encourages deeper communication and intimacy, fostering an environment where both partners can explore their desires without shame.

  Tip: This is a moment of trust-building. Make sure both you and your partner feel safe sharing these desires, and create an open, nonjudgmental space for vulnerability. Remember, it's okay if some desires are still being explored—this is part of the process.

- **Activity 2: Exploring New Desires Together**
  After sharing your desires, choose one to explore together. Start small, ensuring that both of you are comfortable and clear about your boundaries. Allow yourselves to experiment and discover new aspects of your dynamic. This can involve trying something new in the bedroom, exploring a different type of roleplay, or incorporating new rituals or activities into your relationship. The goal is to create an environment where both of you feel supported and encouraged to explore new facets of your desires.

  Tip: As you explore these new desires, check in with each other throughout the experience. This helps to maintain clear communication and ensure that both of you are comfortable with the progression of your exploration.

- **Activity 3: Journaling Desire's Role in Your Dynamic**
  Reflect on the desires that have surfaced in your journey. Write about how they have evolved and how you and your partner have explored them together. What new desires have emerged, and how are they expressed or explored? Are there desires that you're still working to understand or communicate clearly? Use this journaling practice to track your growth and emotional shifts as you discover more about your desires and how they relate to your relationship.

  Tip: As you journal, be honest with yourself. Your desires may evolve, and that's completely normal. Don't rush the process—take time to understand what excites and fulfills you truly.

Journaling Prompt:

1. **What new desires have emerged in my journey, and how are they being explored?** Reflect on the desires that have developed over time. Are there things that you're now open to exploring that once felt off-limits? Write about how your desires have changed and how you approach them in a way that feels true to you and your dynamic.

2. **How do my desires contribute to my emotional and physical intimacy with my partner?** Consider how your desires affect your connection. Do they bring you closer together, or do they require deeper communication and understanding? Reflect on how they play a role in strengthening your bond.

3. **How do I communicate my desires to my partner healthily?** Write about sharing your desires with your partner and how this communication shapes your dynamic. Are there areas where you want to improve in expressing what you want? How can you foster a safe space to discuss desires without fear of judgment?

Closing Reflection:

Desire is a powerful force that can lead you to deeper connection and self-discovery. By taking the time to explore your desires through introspection and sharing them with your partner, you not only enhance your relationship but also deepen your understanding of yourself.

Allowing yourself to be vulnerable in expressing your desires creates trust and intimacy. It's an opportunity to align your emotional and physical needs, ensuring both partners feel heard and fulfilled. Remember, desires evolve, and it's essential to approach them with openness, curiosity, and respect.

By honoring your desires and your partner's, you create a dynamic where exploration and growth are encouraged, and both partners can feel free to be their authentic selves.

Personal Reflections:

The Balance of Giving and Receiving

Meditation:

Find a comfortable, quiet space to relax and close your eyes. Take several deep breaths, inhaling slowly through your nose, holding for a moment, and then exhaling gently through your mouth. Allow yourself to release any tension and become fully present in this moment.

Now, visualize a circle, a continuous loop of giving and receiving. Picture this circle as an energetic exchange between you and your partner. See the flow of energy moving seamlessly back and forth, with each act of giving creating space for receiving and each act of receiving deepening the flow of giving. Reflect on how balanced the exchange feels—there's no pressure to give more than what is comfortable and no hesitation in receiving what is offered.

Consider how giving can be a powerful expression of care and leadership and how receiving allows space for vulnerability and trust. In this balance, giving and receiving are essential; each enhances the other. What does it look like when this flow is perfectly balanced, and how does it feel in your dynamic?

Affirmation:
I honor the sacred flow of energy between giving and receiving. In this balance, I find strength, connection, and trust.

Practices in Action:

- **Activity 1: Giving and Receiving Flow**
  Engage in an activity where you alternate between giving and receiving. This could be something simple like offering a massage and then allowing your partner to give one in return, or perhaps a moment of care and attention where you alternate between showing affection and receiving it. Focus on how the energy flow feels—does it feel natural and effortless? Or do you notice any hesitation or discomfort at any point?

  Tip: Pay attention to any imbalances that may arise. Are you more comfortable giving than receiving, or vice versa? This activity can help you realize where you might be holding back in the dynamic. The goal is to practice both sides of the exchange with complete openness and presence.

- **Activity 2: Ritual of Mutual Care**
  Create a small ritual where you and your partner alternate roles, offering and receiving care differently. For example, you might take turns planning and executing an activity that nurtures the other, whether sensual or emotionally grounding. This can be a simple exchange, like preparing a comforting meal for your partner and then receiving a gesture of care from them in return.

Tip: The key is to recognize that both giving and receiving contribute to the emotional depth of the relationship. When one partner always gives without allowing the other to contribute, the flow can become strained. Work toward a balanced exchange of energy, support, and nurturing in this exercise.

- **Activity 3: Journaling Your Experience**
  After engaging in a session of giving and receiving, take some time to journal your experience. Reflect on how the balance of energy felt. Were there moments when you felt more comfortable giving than receiving? Did you feel open to receiving, or did it take effort? How did this experience affect the emotional connection between you and your partner?

  Tip: Be honest in your reflection. If there are areas where you felt discomfort or reluctance, explore why that might be. Do you struggle with letting your guard down to receive, or are there moments when you feel too overwhelmed to give? Journaling is a great way to uncover deeper patterns and work toward a more harmonious dynamic.

Journaling Prompts:

1. **What does the balance of giving and receiving look like in my dynamic?** Reflect on the moments when you've noticed the energy exchange flowing smoothly. Are there particular aspects of your relationship where you feel a natural rhythm of giving and receiving? How do you support each other in these areas?

2. **When I give, what emotions arise for me?** Consider what giving feels like—do you feel empowered, caring, or perhaps vulnerable? Reflect on the positive emotions that arise when you offer something to your partner, whether it's love, attention, or care.

3. **When I receive it, how do I feel?** Explore how receiving feels—are you comfortable, or do you feel guilt or hesitation? Do you feel honored when your partner gives to you? Write about your feelings of receiving and how they impact your connection.

4. **How can I improve the energy flow between giving and receiving?** If you notice any imbalances in your dynamic, reflect on what changes you can make to improve energy flow. Are you giving too much without allowing your partner to give back? Or are you struggling to allow yourself to receive? How can you create a more harmonious exchange?

Closing Reflection:

The balance of giving and receiving is vital to any relationship, particularly in a dynamic where both partners are deeply attuned to each other's needs. This exchange of energy fosters trust, connection, and intimacy. When both partners feel free to give and receive without hesitation or imbalance, the dynamic becomes a powerful source of mutual growth.

By engaging in practices that reinforce this balance, you cultivate a relationship based on reciprocity, where both partners contribute to the emotional and physical well-being of the other. The more you embrace this flow, the deeper your connection will become, creating a dynamic rooted in respect, care, and understanding.

Personal Reflections:

The Role of Dominance in Everyday Life

Meditation:

Take a moment to find a comfortable position in a chair or on the floor. Close your eyes and breathe deeply, letting go of distractions around you. Allow yourself to become present in this moment.

Now, begin to reflect on how dominance can be embodied in the everyday moments of life beyond the play and scene. Consider how small actions—like communicating, making decisions, or leading—reflect your dominant role. Picture how dominance feels when you decide on your own or guide your partner through daily tasks. It's not just about controlling or commanding; it's about the power you bring through confidence, attentiveness, and care.

Visualize your dominance as a constant, steady force—whether managing a task, taking charge in a conversation, or making choices that benefit you and your partner. How do these everyday acts shape your dynamic? How does exercising dominance in mundane actions influence the more profound understanding of your role?

Affirmation:
I embody dominance with care, attention, and confidence in all aspects of my life. I am a guide and protector, not just in moments of play but in the everyday rhythm of our relationship.

Practices in Action:

- **Activity 1: Daily Decision-Making**
  For the day, take the lead in big and small decision-making. This could be as simple as choosing where to eat or making more significant decisions affecting your shared life. The goal is to practice your dominance by taking the initiative and considering how these choices affect your partner and your dynamic. Let your partner trust your guidance in making decisions.

  Tip: As you make decisions, check in with yourself and reflect on how you're embodying your dominance. Are you doing so confidently, with the intention of benefiting both yourself and your partner? Are you also mindful of your partner's needs as you lead? Practice patience and awareness as you lead throughout the day.

- **Activity 2: Lead with Responsibility**
  Take charge of a task or responsibility shared between you and your partner. This could be a chore, a project, or a decision regarding your shared living space. By stepping up and taking the lead, you reinforce your dominant role, showing that dominance is not about control but responsibility and mutual respect.

Tip: As you assume responsibility, ensure you are still receptive to your partner's input and feelings. Dominance in everyday life isn't about ignoring your partner's perspective but instead incorporating their needs into your decisions. Take note of how your leadership influences the dynamic and fosters trust in mundane and extraordinary moments.

- **Activity 3: Journal Your Reflection**
  Reflect on how you exercised dominance in everyday life. Consider your choices, how you led, and how your partner responded. Did you feel a deeper connection or understanding of your role as a Dominant? Did the responsibility of everyday leadership feel different than during scenes or play?

  Tip: Use journaling to explore how dominance in day-to-day life strengthens your connection with your partner. Are there moments where you felt more grounded in your role? Are there areas where you found challenges? Write about how these everyday moments influence the broader dynamics in your relationship.

Journaling Prompts:

1. **How do I express dominance in my daily life?**
   Reflect on your natural habits of dominance in everyday moments. Do you take charge when needed, or do you hesitate? How do you lead in situations outside of play, and how does it feel when you step into this role?

2. **What responsibilities come with dominance in everyday life?**
   Dominance isn't just about control; it's about responsibility. How do you handle the responsibilities that come with leading? Are you conscious of how your choices affect both you and your partner? Explore how you balance your dominant role with your need for self-care and awareness of your partner's needs.

3. **How does leading in everyday life deepen my understanding of dominance?**
   Reflect on the connection between everyday acts of leadership and your understanding of dominance. How does it feel to exercise control outside of play scenarios? How does this enhance your sense of responsibility and your role as a Dominant partner?

4. **What challenges arise when I lead in everyday life?**
   Consider moments when you felt hesitant or unsure about taking charge. Are there situations where you find it difficult to exercise dominance? Reflect on how to work through those moments to strengthen your confidence in your role.

Closing Reflection:

Dominance is not confined to playtime or scenes—it is woven into the everyday moments that define the relationship. By taking the lead in decision-making, responsibility, and care, you reinforce the power dynamic in ways that go beyond physical acts. It's about embodying your role with confidence, awareness, and respect for your partner.

When dominance is practiced in everyday life, it cultivates a deeper understanding of the role—one that is grounded in responsibility, trust, and mutual growth. The more you step into your dominant role throughout your life, the stronger the emotional and psychological connection between you and your partner.

Personal Reflections:

Exploring Emotional Reactions to Pain

Meditation:

Find a comfortable, seated position, close your eyes, and breathe deeply. Feel your body relax, exhale, and release any tension with each inhale. Allow your mind to become present and focused.

Now, focus on the physical sensations of pain. This could be a mild ache, discomfort, or something more intense. Rather than resisting it, allow yourself to sit with it and observe it. Notice the emotional reactions that come with pain—does it trigger frustration, clarity, excitement, or something else entirely?

Pain, whether physical or emotional, is often tied to deeper feelings, and it's important to acknowledge how it manifests within your dynamic. As you explore pain sensations, reflect on how it affects your sense of control, responsibility, and trust. Does the pain create a deeper connection or understanding between you and your partner? Does it reveal something about your emotional landscape that you hadn't noticed before?

Affirmation:
I acknowledge the emotional complexity of pain and use it as a tool for deeper understanding and connection in my role. I lead with care, respect, and clear communication, ensuring pain is handled thoughtfully and safely.

Practices in Action:

- **Activity 1: Pain Boundaries and Communication**
  Discuss openly with your partner about how pain is experienced and communicated in your dynamic. What physical or emotional boundaries do you have when it comes to pain? Are there particular triggers or limits that should be respected? Talk about how you both feel during moments of pain and what methods of communication work best—whether it's a safe word, gesture, or verbal check-ins.

  Tip: As a Dominant, it's essential to be aware of your partner's emotional and physical state during moments of pain. Practice using a calm, reassuring voice when discussing pain, and listen actively to your partner's concerns. Pain is not just about physical sensation but the emotional context surrounding it, so be attuned to how your partner feels in those moments.

- **Activity 2: Roleplaying Pain Communication**
  Engage in a light roleplay scenario where you explore the experience of pain. One of you can pretend to experience discomfort (either physical or emotional), and the other can practice how they would respond. How do you maintain control and reassurance during these moments? Practice guiding your partner through the discomfort, ensuring they feel heard and cared for. Remember, pain should never be used as a punishment but as a tool for growth and connection.

Tip: Roleplay in a way that allows both of you to express what feels safe and comfortable and experiment with different ways of communicating pain. Are there particular words or cues that help ease the experience, or do you need to adjust the approach based on each person's needs?

- **Activity 3: Journaling Reflection**
  After reflecting on the role of pain in your dynamic, write a journal about your emotional connection to pain. What do you feel when experiencing pain, and how does it differ from how your partner experiences it? Explore how pain has been used to connect or strengthen your relationship and how you communicate during these moments.

  Tip: Be honest with yourself in your journaling. Is there discomfort with pain you must work through, or is it a space where you find growth? Use this journal entry to explore your emotional reactions when pain is present and how you can better support your partner through it.

Journaling Prompts:

1. **How do I react emotionally to pain in my dynamic?**
   Reflect on how you emotionally process pain when you experience it and guide your partner through it. Does it evoke empathy, control, discomfort, or something else? How does your emotional reaction impact the experience as a whole?

2. **What boundaries should we maintain regarding pain?**
   Explore what hard limits and soft limits exist around pain in your dynamic. What physical or emotional boundaries must be respected, and how do you navigate them together? Are there specific guidelines that help both of you feel safe and cared for during moments of discomfort?

3. **How does pain enhance our connection, and how can we use it for growth?**
   Think about moments when physical or emotional pain has deepened your connection. How does it shift the dynamic, and how do you use it as an opportunity for growth? Reflect on how you, as the Dominant, can help guide your partner through these moments to ensure they feel supported and safe.

4. **What emotional triggers come up for me during moments of pain?**
   Pain often stirs deeper emotions. Do you find yourself experiencing frustration, anger, guilt, or other emotions? Explore how these emotional triggers manifest during pain and how to use them to enhance your understanding of your feelings and your partner's needs.

Closing Reflection:

Pain, when experienced mindfully and communicated effectively, can be a powerful tool in deepening the bond between you and your partner. It's not about causing harm but about guiding each other through discomfort to foster trust, communication, and connection.

As a Dominant, you are responsible for ensuring that any moments of pain are handled with care, respect, and clear communication. By understanding how pain impacts both you and your partner on an emotional level, you create a space where vulnerability and trust can flourish. Through your actions and words, you provide a framework where pain becomes a catalyst for deeper connection and growth rather than a source of fear or harm.

Personal Reflections:

Releasing Stress Through Power Exchange

Meditation:

Find a comfortable, seated position and take a deep breath, filling your lungs completely. Then, exhale slowly, releasing any tension. With each breath, allow your body to relax deeper into the moment.

Visualize the stress and pressures of the day as a heavy weight you carry. See it in your mind's eye: perhaps as a dark cloud or a weight on your shoulders. Now, imagine this weight slowly lifting as you focus on your dynamic. Picture the power exchange between you and your partner as a force that helps you release all the accumulated stress like a gentle stream washing away dirt. As you give your control to the situation, allow your tension and worries to dissolve into the energy between you and your partner. Feel the relief of surrendering to the world's pressures, letting your dynamic be a source of peace, connection, and restoration.

Affirmation:
I allow the power exchange to be a tool for releasing the stresses of my day. Through this dynamic, I create space for relaxation, healing, and restoration for myself and my partner.

Practices in Action:

- **Activity 1: Stress-Relief Focused Session**
  Plan a session where the primary goal is to release stress through the power exchange. It could involve a physical practice like massage or relaxation techniques or focus on emotional release through a structured play session. The key is to create a safe, calm environment where both partners can let go of external pressures. The session should focus on relaxation, mutual trust, and the emotional cleansing that occurs when stress is released.

  Tip: As the Dominant, focus on guiding the session with clear communication and reassurance. Allow your partner to be vulnerable and let go of their worries, providing a grounding force for them to return to when ready.

- **Activity 2: Breathing Together**
  Spend time focusing on synchronized breathing as a way to release tension together. You can sit across from your partner, placing one hand on their chest and the other on their back. Begin by breathing deeply together, synchronizing your inhales and exhales. With each exhale, visualize releasing the weight of the day's stress and clearing the mental clutter. Let your body relax with each breath, focusing entirely on the moment. This shared rhythm can help you feel connected and grounded in the dynamic, providing a sense of calm from being in tune with each other.

Tip: Make this a routine part of your dynamic, especially after a stressful day. It will help establish a shared relaxation space and foster a sense of partnership and mutual care.

- **Activity 3: Journaling Reflection**
  After the session, write about the experience in a journal. How did it feel to release stress through the dynamic? Did the power exchange help you let go of emotional or physical tension? Reflect on how the power exchange becomes a tool for pleasure and mental and emotional restoration. How does focusing on release during your power exchange activities change how you experience the dynamic?

  Tip: Pay attention to how the release of stress impacts your emotional state and the strength of your connection with your partner. It might help to focus on specific moments where you felt exceptionally relaxed or at ease. This can give you insight into how the dynamic can be a vital tool.

Journaling Prompts:

1. **What stressors did I release during our dynamic?**
   Reflect on the external stress that you carried before the session. How did engaging in power exchange help to release those pressures? What specific actions, words, or moments during the session helped you relax and let go?

2. **How does the act of surrendering control aid in stress release?**
   Think about the emotional and physical sensations you experienced while releasing control. How does surrendering feel like a form of stress release? How do you balance this surrender with maintaining leadership in the dynamic?

3. **How does engaging in power exchange offer mental and emotional restoration?**
   Consider how engaging in power exchange creates a space of relaxation. Does the trust and connection fostered by the dynamic help you release physical tension and mental and emotional stress as well? How does it shift your perspective after a stressful time?

4. **What do I need in these moments of stress release?**
   Reflect on your personal needs during these stress-relieving activities. Do you need guidance, reassurance, or something else to feel entirely relaxed? How can you communicate these needs to your partner for a more effective stress release?

Closing Reflection:

The power exchange dynamic offers a unique opportunity to release physical and emotional stress. By creating a structured space where control can be surrendered, and trust can be built, both partners can experience the freedom of letting go. Stress doesn't have to be carried alone; you can offer each other relief and restoration through power exchange.

As the Dominant, you play a pivotal role in guiding this release process, creating an environment that allows both of you to find peace and relaxation. Power exchange is not just a tool for pleasure but also a method for healing, grounding, and rejuvenating the mind and body. By embracing this, you strengthen your dynamic and foster a sense of balance and well-being in both partners.

Personal Reflections:

Cultivating Patience in the Dynamic

Meditation:

Sit in a comfortable, quiet space where you can focus without interruption. Close your eyes and take a deep breath, feeling the air fill your lungs and release. With each breath, allow your body to relax and your mind to quiet.

Now, focus on the concept of patience. Picture it as a force that flows slowly and steadily between you and your partner. It isn't rushed or forced—it's a profound, calm energy that allows things to unfold naturally. As you visualize this patience, imagine it deepening the bond between you and your submissive, creating space for connection without pressure. How does patience feel in your body? Do you think it is in the steady rhythm of your breath or the quiet stillness of your mind?

Patience doesn't just mean waiting; it means allowing your dynamic to unfold at its own pace, nurturing it carefully with intention. Embrace the quiet power of patience, knowing that each moment of waiting builds trust and connection.

Affirmation:
I embrace the strength of patience, allowing it to deepen my connection with my submissive. Through patience, we grow closer, building trust and intimacy with every step.

Practices in Action:

- **Activity 1: Slow and Intentional Scene**
  Engage in a scene where the focus is on slow, deliberate actions. Take your time guiding your submissive through each step, paying attention to their reactions and needs. This practice emphasizes the importance of patience, showing that connection is built not on quick, reactive actions but through careful, thoughtful leadership.

  Tip: Use verbal and non-verbal cues to help the submissive remain in the moment. Patience in your leadership will help them feel safe and cared for as they move through each step of the scene. This slow pace may heighten the intensity and deepen the trust between you both.

- **Activity 2: Guide Through Every Step**
  During your scene, offer gentle guidance for each action, from breathing exercises to movements. Focus on giving clear, calm instructions and give your partner ample time to respond. This exercise can be an opportunity to practice patience not just in action but also in communication. By being intentional with every step, you show your submissives that they are supported and not rushed.

Tip: When guiding your partner, focus on their emotional and physical state, asking for feedback to ensure comfort and understanding. Your patience will show them they can trust you to lead with care, creating a deeper bond of respect and intimacy.

- **Activity 3: Journaling Reflection**
  After the scene, take time to reflect on the experience. Write about how patience played a role in the dynamic. Did you notice moments where you felt compelled to rush but chose to slow down instead? How did that impact the connection between you and your submissive? Reflect on how patience deepens trust and intimacy in your dynamic and how it may have transformed your experience of the scene.

  Tip: Consider what moments felt particularly powerful because of your cultivated patience. Did the slow pace make you feel more connected to your partner, or did it lead to discoveries about your dynamic?

Journaling Prompts:

1. **How does patience impact my ability to connect with my submissive?**
   Reflect on moments in your dynamic where patience has deepened your bond. How does the slow unfolding of the relationship or scene allow for greater intimacy? How does it foster trust?

2. **In what ways does slowing down enhance the power dynamic?**
   Think about how a slower, more intentional approach might change the experience for both of you. How does taking your time with each step—emotionally or physically—create space for a deeper connection?

3. **What challenges do I face when practicing patience, and how do I overcome them?**
   Reflect on times when patience was challenging to practice. Was there a sense of urgency or a desire for immediate gratification that got in the way? How did you manage those feelings, and what did you learn from them?

4. **How does patience build trust and intimacy in my dynamic?**
   Be patient with your partner's needs, reactions, and responses, strengthening your bond. Does patience provide the space for vulnerability, and how does it promote emotional closeness?

Closing Reflection:

Patience is often underappreciated in a dynamic, but its power cannot be overstated. It provides the space for connection, growth, and deep emotional intimacy. Through patience, both partners can feel honestly heard and supported, which leads to a stronger bond and a more meaningful exchange of power.

As the Dominant, your ability to slow down and guide with intention speaks volumes about your care and respect for your submissive. In a fast-paced world, cultivating patience in your dynamic becomes an act of love. You genuinely connect in these slow, deliberate moments; in those moments, you'll find trust, intimacy, and connection flourishing.

Personal Reflections:

Forgiveness and Letting Go of Guilt

Meditation:

Sit comfortably and close your eyes, allowing your breath to slow and deepen. Focus on the sensation of your breath filling your chest and expanding your lungs. With each exhale, let go of any tension you may be holding.

Now, shift your focus to forgiveness. Imagine a warm, healing light radiating from your heart, surrounding any feelings of guilt or shame. These emotions can be heavy, but forgiveness transforms them. Picture this light gently dissolving guilt, replacing it with growth, understanding, and compassion.

Reflect on a time in your relationship when forgiveness was needed—whether within the context of your dynamic or outside of it. How did forgiving yourself and your partner allow your relationship to evolve? How does it feel to release the weight of guilt, knowing it only hinders your growth together?

Affirmation:
I forgive myself and my partner, letting go of guilt and allowing our dynamic to flourish with love, trust, and mutual respect. Forgiveness is the path to deeper connection and growth.

Practices in Action:

- **Activity 1: Open Conversation About Past Mistakes**
  If a boundary has been unintentionally crossed, it's important to address it openly, without shame or blame. Create a space where both partners can speak honestly about what happened, how it felt, and what can be learned from the experience. Acknowledge any feelings of guilt and work together to release them, focusing on the understanding and forgiveness that will strengthen your relationship moving forward.

  Tip: Approach the conversation with compassion, listening carefully and speaking from a place of vulnerability. The goal is to heal and grow, not to place blame. This practice will reinforce the idea that mistakes are part of the learning process, not something to be feared.

- **Activity 2: Release and Reframe Guilt**
  Reflect on any guilt you may carry within the dynamic, especially if it's been tied to mistakes or missteps. Visualize releasing these feelings, allowing them to flow out of your body like dark smoke. Replace the guilt with a sense of growth, understanding that the mistakes made are stepping stones to a stronger, more resilient relationship. Engage with your partner about how you can actively support each other in letting go of guilt and turning it into an opportunity for a deeper connection.

Tip: Offer affirmations to each other, reinforcing that you are not defined by past mistakes but by the love and growth you share in the present moment.

- **Activity 3: Journaling Reflection**
  After the practice, take a moment to reflect on forgiveness. Write about how guilt has impacted your relationship in the past and how forgiveness has transformed those moments. How has forgiveness deepened your trust in one another? How has it allowed your dynamic to evolve and grow stronger? Reflect on how releasing guilt has allowed you to be more present in your relationship, both inside and outside of BDSM play.

  Tip: Consider what steps you can take to make forgiveness a more natural part of your dynamic. What new rituals or practices can you incorporate to help release guilt when it arises?

Journaling Prompts:

1. **How do I feel when I forgive myself and my partner?**
   Reflect on the emotional release that comes with letting go of guilt. How does forgiveness allow you to move forward with a renewed sense of connection?

2. **What role does forgiveness play in healing after a boundary is crossed?**
   Consider how forgiveness helps rebuild trust after a mistake. How does it provide the space to reconnect and deepen your bond?

3. **How can I create a space for open, shame-free conversations in our dynamic?**
   Think about ways to encourage open dialogue when things are unplanned. How can you establish trust that makes it easier to address any issues without fear of judgment?

4. **How does forgiving myself or my partner impact how I approach future scenes or emotional moments?**
   Reflect on how forgiveness can enhance your understanding of your partner's needs and your role in the dynamic. How does releasing guilt contribute to a healthier, more vibrant connection?

Closing Reflection:

Forgiveness is a powerful tool in any relationship, especially in the context of BDSM dynamics. It allows both partners to release any weight that holds them back, creating space for healing, growth, and deeper connection. Forgiving yourself and your partner doesn't mean forgetting mistakes; it means understanding that mistakes are part of the journey toward a stronger, more resilient bond.

In BDSM, where trust is paramount, forgiving and letting go of guilt becomes a vital step in building a deep and lasting connection. It reminds us that we are not defined by our errors but by our commitment to each other's growth, understanding, and mutual respect. By cultivating forgiveness, we embrace a dynamic full of love, care, and the freedom to be vulnerable without fear of judgment.

Personal Reflections:

Reaffirming Roles Through Ritual

Meditation:

Sit comfortably and close your eyes. Take a few deep breaths, grounding yourself in the present moment. Inhale deeply, fill your lungs, and exhale slowly, releasing tension or distractions. Allow your breath to become slow and steady.

Now, envision a ritual where the roles of Dominant and submissive are powerfully reinforced. Picture yourself stepping into the role of the Dominant, feeling the weight of responsibility and authority. How does it feel to assume this position? Do you feel a sense of power, clarity, or even vulnerability as you hold space for your submissive?

Imagine your submissive embracing their role as well, surrendering to the trust and connection you've built together. How does this dynamic make you feel more aligned, connected, and present with each other?

Reaffirming your roles through ritual creates a sense of structure and sacredness within your dynamic. Let this visualization guide you in exploring what these roles mean and how they bring you closer.

Affirmation:
I step into my role as a Dominant with purpose, honor, and respect. I embrace the responsibility and power of guiding and nurturing my submissive. Through ritual, we strengthen our connection and affirm the bond we share.

Practices in Action:

- **Activity 1: Ritual Creation**
  Rituals can be a powerful way to reaffirm your roles within your dynamic, especially if they are simple and meaningful. Work together to create a ritual that feels authentic to your relationship. This might include a collaring ceremony, an affirmation exchange, or a service ritual where the submissive offers a gesture of respect to the Dominant.

  Tip: Focus the ritual on the significance of your roles, how they reinforce trust, and how they create a sense of emotional safety and belonging. Feelings of connection and respect will also be important as you engage in this shared experience.

- **Activity 2: Role-Playing Rituals**
  Another way to strengthen the roles in your dynamic is to roleplay the ritual in a way that highlights both power and surrender. Engage in a scene where the Dominant leads with clear intent and the submissive willingly surrenders, reinforcing your role's sacredness and power.

Tip: Be intentional about transitioning into and out of the ritual. The beginning and end of the ritual should feel just as meaningful as the act itself. You might want to incorporate words of affirmation, quiet reflection, or a simple physical gesture that solidifies the moment.

- **Activity 3: Journaling Reflection**
  After completing your ritual, take time to reflect on its impact. How did it feel to step into your role as Dominant or submissive during the ritual? What emotions surfaced for both of you? Did the ritual make your connection feel more profound, meaningful, or secure?

  Tip: Write about how this ritual changes the way you view your role in the dynamic. Does it bring a new layer of appreciation or understanding? Does it reinforce your connection, your commitment, or the trust between you? How does ritual help you feel more grounded in your relationship?

Journaling Prompts:

1. **How does stepping into my role as Dominant make me feel?**
   Reflect on the emotions you experience when you assume your role. Do you feel empowered, responsible, vulnerable, or something else? How does this feeling strengthen your relationship?

2. **What does my submissive role mean to me, and how do I honor it?**
   Consider the significance of your submissive's role in the dynamic. What responsibilities or commitments do you hold to ensure that they feel respected and cared for within their role?

3. **How does ritual create structure and sacredness in our dynamic?**
   Reflect on how ritual reinforces the emotional and spiritual aspects of your relationship. Does it create a more profound sense of trust, intimacy, or meaning?

4. **What new rituals could we create to strengthen our dynamic and reaffirm our roles?**
   Brainstorm new rituals or practices that can deepen your connection. How can you continue to honor your roles through meaningful and intentional actions?

Closing Reflection:

Rituals are a powerful way to reaffirm and reinforce the roles within a Dominant/submissive dynamic. They provide structure and meaning, allowing both partners to step into their roles with clarity and intention. Whether through something as formal as a collaring ceremony or something as simple as an affirmation exchange, rituals help deepen trust, reinforce respect, and create a sense of emotional safety.

For the Dominant, rituals are an opportunity to fully embrace the responsibility and power of the role fully, guiding and nurturing the submissive with care and intent. For the submissive, rituals offer a moment of surrender, reinforcing the trust and vulnerability essential to the dynamic.

By engaging in these rituals, both partners create a shared experience that brings them closer together, strengthening their emotional connection and commitment to each other.

Personal Reflections:

The Connection Between Pain and Pleasure

Meditation:

Find a comfortable place to sit or lie down. Close your eyes, taking slow, deliberate breaths. With each inhale, feel yourself becoming more present in the moment; release any lingering tension with each exhale.

Now, bring your awareness to the physical sensations of pain and pleasure. Imagine the two sensations side by side, how they might feel distinct yet intertwined. Consider how your body reacts to both pain and pleasure, individually and together. Do they think like opposites or blend to create something more profound?

Explore how these sensations coexist for you. Does pain intensify pleasure, or does pleasure soften pain? Reflect on how you experience this dynamic in your relationship, knowing that both elements play a role in deepening connection and intimacy.

Affirmation:
I honor the interplay between pain and pleasure, embracing how they weave together to deepen our connection. I lead with intention, always respecting the boundaries and desires of my submissive as we explore these sensations.

Practices in Action:

- **Activity 1: Controlled Exploration of Pain and Pleasure**
  In your next scene, introduce pain and pleasure in a controlled, mindful way. Start slow, testing the waters of both sensations. For example, the Dominant might administer light spanks or pressure and simultaneously engage in the form of touch that induces pleasure, like gentle caresses or kisses.

  Tip: Be mindful of communication throughout the scene. Pay attention to your submissive's physical responses and verbal cues, ensuring that the balance between pain and pleasure remains positive and consensual. Consider using words of affirmation, praise, or encouragement to amplify the connection.

- **Activity 2: Sensory Play with Boundaries**
  Sensory play is a powerful way to explore the balance between pain and pleasure. Use tools like feathers, ice, or wax to stimulate the skin differently. Allow these sensations to evolve, guiding your submissive through each change carefully. As a Dominant, use your intuition to gauge how your submissive is responding to both pain and pleasure.

  Tip: Throughout this activity, be especially tuned into your submissive's physical and emotional responses. Check-in with them, either verbally or through subtle cues, to ensure that the pain and pleasure elements are experienced positively and enrichingly.

- **Activity 3: Reaffirming Boundaries During Pain/Pleasure Play**
  While exploring the connection between pain and pleasure, constantly reaffirm your boundaries and expectations. Create a safe space where both partners can communicate openly during the scene. Use safe words or gestures to indicate when something is too much or when they want to adjust the intensity.

  Tip: Setting clear boundaries beforehand ensures that both partners can relax into the experience, knowing that any shift in the dynamic will be respected. Reinforce trust by demonstrating that the Dominant will always honor these limits.

Journaling Prompts:

1. **How do I experience the connection between pain and pleasure?**
   Reflect on how these sensations manifest for you. Do they feel like two separate experiences, or do they overlap and enhance each other in specific moments? How do they impact your emotional and physical state?

2. **How do I introduce both pain and pleasure in a way that's mindful and consensual?**
   Consider the steps you take to guide your submissive through these sensations. How do you ensure the experience feels safe and fulfilling for both of you?

3. **How does intertwining pain and pleasure affect our emotional connection?**
   Reflect on moments where pain and pleasure have converged. What emotional shifts occurred during these moments? Did it create a deeper bond, greater vulnerability, or a sense of shared intimacy?

4. **What lessons have I learned from exploring pain and pleasure together?**
   Consider how this exploration has changed your dynamic, both physically and emotionally. What have you discovered about your needs, desires, and limits through this practice?

Closing Reflection:

The connection between pain and pleasure is a unique and deeply personal aspect of a Dominant/submissive relationship. For many, the interplay between these sensations can amplify the emotional and physical connection, creating an intense and nurturing dynamic.

As a Dominant, your role is to guide your submissive through these experiences, ensuring that both pain and pleasure are experienced in a safe, consensual, and respectful way. You hold the responsibility to maintain balance and to be attuned to your submissive's emotional and physical responses.

Exploring the synergy between pain and pleasure can deepen your dynamic's trust and intimacy, helping you grow individually and as partners. By honoring the connection between these sensations, you create space for new forms of pleasure and emotional connection to flourish.

Personal Reflections:

Personal Growth Through Submission

Meditation:

Find a quiet space where you can sit comfortably. Close your eyes and take a few deep breaths, grounding yourself in the present moment. With each inhale, feel calmness filling your body; with each exhale, release any tension.

Now, focus on the concept of submission as a tool for personal growth. Visualize how emotional, physical, or mental surrender can lead to deeper understanding and transformation. What lessons can be learned through submission, both for your submissive and for yourself as a Dominant? Consider how your role in guiding them can facilitate their growth and how this process allows you to evolve together.

Think about the areas in which submission challenges your submissive to step beyond their limits or embrace vulnerability. How does their growth enhance the dynamic between you? Reflect on how this act of submission can be a journey of personal empowerment, both for the submissive and the Dominant.

Affirmation:
Through submission, my partner and I grow. I embrace my role in nurturing their growth and honor the lessons that submission brings to our dynamic.

Practices in Action:

- **Activity 1: Exploring New Aspects of Submission**
  Encourage your submissive to step into a new aspect of their role that challenges them to grow. This could involve more profound emotional vulnerability, new physical challenges, or embracing a new power dynamic. As the Dominant, guide them with care and respect, helping them explore these areas while ensuring they feel safe and supported.

  Tip: Encourage your submissive to share their thoughts and feelings about their growth. This can help you understand what they are learning from their submission and how they feel during the experience.

- **Activity 2: Mental and Emotional Challenges**
  Submission can also involve mental and emotional challenges that lead to growth. For example, you may ask your submissive to practice mindfulness or meditation or explore a scenario where they must let go of control mentally. As the Dominant, ensure that the challenge is constructive and that you align with expectations.

  Tip: Frame the activity as an opportunity for growth rather than just a role-playing exercise. Highlight how each step taken in submission contributes to both of your journeys.

- **Activity 3: Reflecting on Lessons Learned**
  After a scene or dynamic experience, take time to reflect together on the lessons learned. Have your submissive share how they felt during the experience and what personal growth they noticed. As a Dominant, reflect on how you supported their journey and what you learned from the interaction.

  Tip: Create space for open dialogue about how submission has affected both of you emotionally and mentally. This reflection can deepen your emotional connection and help you both process the growth that has occurred.

Journaling Prompts:

1. **How does submission challenge me to grow mentally and emotionally?**
   Reflect on how the submissive role requires you to go beyond surface-level desires and tap into deeper emotional or mental growth aspects. How does surrender influence your understanding of yourself and others?

2. **In what ways has submission helped me become more self-aware?**
   Submission often requires introspection, as it involves vulnerability and trust. How has stepping into this dynamic helped you understand your emotional needs, boundaries, or desires more deeply?

3. **What lessons have I learned about control, trust, and vulnerability through submission?**
   Submission can be a powerful way to explore your relationship with control and trust. What have you learned about both yourself and your submissive through these experiences? How have those lessons shaped your dynamic?

4. **How can I support my partner's growth through their submission?**
   As a Dominant, you have the responsibility to guide your submissive's growth. What actions or behaviors can you take to ensure that submission becomes a positive tool for personal development? How can you reinforce their progress and encourage more profound growth?

Closing Reflection:

Submission is a deeply personal and transformative process. It's an opportunity for the submissive to explore vulnerability, trust, and growth, often in ways they haven't experienced before. For the Dominant, guiding a submissive through this process can lead to a deeper understanding of their desires and motivations while nurturing their partner's emotional and mental development.

Through submission, both partners are invited to evolve, not just within the dynamic but as individuals. The act of surrender becomes a tool for personal empowerment and growth. When approached with intention and care, submission becomes a powerful pathway to self-discovery, fostering a deeper connection and understanding between partners.

The Sub

The Submissive Partner

In the world of power exchange, the submissive's role is often misunderstood or overlooked. However, it is just as vital and nuanced as that of the Dominant. For the submissive, submission is not about weakness or passivity; instead, it is an active, conscious choice to surrender power in a trusting and intentional way. It is about finding strength in vulnerability, deepening connection, and exploring the depths of personal growth through surrender.

Submission is not one-size-fits-all. It is a personal journey between autonomy and trust, where the submissive can explore their emotions, desires, and boundaries in a space of safety, respect, and care. It is an act of trust—not just in the Dominant but oneself. To submit is to understand your needs, acknowledge your limits, and, ultimately, find liberation in the release of control.

As a submissive, your power lies not in compliance alone but in the clarity you express your desires, the boundaries you set, and the trust you place in your partner. You are an equal participant in this dynamic, and your voice, emotions, and well-being are equally significant. Submission requires profound self-awareness, introspection, and a willingness to grow emotionally and physically.

This section invites you to explore the world of submission from a deeply personal perspective. You will be guided through meditations, practices, and reflections that help you uncover the layers of your desires, the meaning behind your submission, and how this dynamic can foster personal growth, emotional connection, and intimacy. Each practice aims to deepen your understanding of what it means to surrender, how it can empower you, and how to navigate this journey in a healthy, fulfilling, and respectful way.

Embracing Vulnerability in Submission

Meditation:

Find a quiet space where you can sit comfortably. Close your eyes and take a few deep breaths, grounding yourself in the present moment. With each inhale, feel calmness filling your body; with each exhale, release any tension.

Now, focus on the concept of vulnerability within submission. Visualize how surrendering yourself, emotionally or physically, opens the door to deeper intimacy and trust. Reflect on how vulnerability—without hiding your emotions or desires—creates a space for growth, connection, and understanding. Embrace the strength you find in this vulnerability. How does it shape your submission and deepen your bond with your Dominant?

Think about how being vulnerable in your submission impacts you and your Dominant. How does it create a stronger emotional and spiritual connection? Reflect on the power of this surrender and how it makes you feel more alive, more seen, and more deeply connected in your dynamic.

Affirmation:
I am strong in my vulnerability. By surrendering and sharing my deepest emotions, I open the door to deeper connection, trust, and growth.

- **Practices in Action**:

  Activity 1: Sharing Vulnerability with Your Dominant
  Choose a time when you feel emotionally open. Share something vulnerable with your Dominant—a feeling, a fear, or a desire that you've been holding back. This could be something as simple as expressing a need for reassurance or something more profound, like a fear of not being enough. Allow yourself to be seen in this moment of emotional openness.

  Tip: Remember, vulnerability doesn't need to be perfect or scripted. The goal is to create an honest exchange that deepens your emotional connection. Let your Dominant hold space for you without judgment.

  Activity 2: Physical Vulnerability
  In a scene, allow yourself to surrender physically, whether in a way that challenges your comfort zone or gives control to your Dominant. Notice how it feels to give up control and let your Dominant lead you. This practice may involve being guided to a point where you are completely open and trusting in your Dominant's hands.

  Tip: Pay attention to how physical vulnerability impacts your emotions. How does it feel to be in a position where you have no control over your body? What feelings arise from this surrender?

Activity 3: Exploring Emotional Boundaries

Discuss with your Dominant where your emotional boundaries lie. What are you afraid of expressing? What emotions or thoughts feel difficult to share? Together, they intend to explore these areas of emotional vulnerability in a safe, supportive way. This is a chance to grow emotionally through trust and open communication.

Tip: Approach this activity with a sense of curiosity. Be open to seeing what you're holding back emotionally, and gently explore the reasons behind it.

- **Journaling Prompts**:

    o How does vulnerability in submission help me grow as an individual?

    o Reflect on how being emotionally or physically vulnerable with your Dominant has deepened your trust. How has it impacted your relationship with yourself and with them?

    o What emotions do I feel when I open up and share something vulnerable? How do these emotions shape my submission and my connection to my Dominant?

    o In what ways does vulnerability bring us closer, and how does it enhance the emotional and spiritual connection between us?

    o How can I fully embrace vulnerability in my submission without fear of judgment or rejection?

Closing Reflection:

Vulnerability in submission is not a weakness but a pathway to profound connection, trust, and growth. By embracing vulnerability, you allow yourself to experience deeper intimacy and open new doors for emotional and spiritual connection with your Dominant. Through this process, submission becomes an act of surrender and a powerful tool for personal empowerment and evolution. When you and your Dominant embrace vulnerability, your dynamic grows more prosperous, meaningful, and full of potential.

Personal Reflections:

The Power of Trust

Meditation:

Find a quiet, comfortable space to sit or lie down. Close your eyes and take a few deep breaths, allowing each breath to relax your body and center your mind. With every inhale, feel yourself becoming more grounded; with every exhale, release any tension.

Now, focus on the concept of trust. Visualize it as a steady anchor deep within you. Picture it as a force that keeps you grounded and secure, even in moments of vulnerability. Think about the trust you place in your Dominant, the belief that they will guide, protect, and lead you in ways that foster your growth. How does it feel to surrender to this trust? How does it shape your submission?

Reflect on the strength of your trust. Trust is not simply about following; it's about feeling safe enough to let go of control and allow your Dominant to guide you. What emotions arise when you place your trust entirely in them? How does this trust create a more profound sense of connection between you?

Affirmation:
I trust my Dominant to lead me with care, respect, and wisdom. I surrender through trust, knowing that it strengthens our bond and deepens our dynamic.

- **Practices in Action**:

  Activity 1: Exploring Trust in New Experiences
  Allow your Dominant to guide you through a new experience where you are unsure or vulnerable. This could be a new type of scene, a new physical or emotional exploration, or even a different interaction that challenges your comfort zone. Focus on your trust in them and how it feels to surrender control in this new territory.

  Tip: Throughout the experience, check in with yourself. What emotions arise when you allow your Dominant to lead you? Does it deepen your connection and trust, or does it bring new challenges to face together?

  Activity 2: Reaffirming Trust During a Scene
  In the middle of a scene, take a moment to pause and connect with your Dominant. Express how you feel in this moment of surrender. How does your trust feel in your body? Are you able to completely relax into your submission because of the trust you have in your Dominant? Let them reassure you if needed, and reflect on the strength of your faith.

  Tip: Use this as an opportunity to communicate non-verbally or verbally, reinforcing that trust through eye contact, physical cues, or words of affirmation. Trust is both an action and an emotion and reaffirming it deepens the experience.

Activity 3: Setting Boundaries with Trust
Trust isn't just about surrendering; it's also about having clear boundaries and knowing that your Dominant will honor them. Take time to discuss and reaffirm your boundaries. How does trust play a role in knowing that your Dominant will respect these limits? How does it feel to express your boundaries freely within the dynamic, knowing that this trust keeps you safe?

Tip: Trust also comes from open communication. Let your Dominant know if anything feels uncomfortable or if a boundary needs to be adjusted. Trust grows stronger when both partners feel safe and heard.

- **Journaling Prompts**:

    o   How does it feel to place my trust in my Dominant? What emotions arise when I allow myself to surrender in this way?

    o   In what ways has trust influenced my submission? How has it deepened my emotional and physical connection with my Dominant?

    o   What does trust look like in my dynamic? Is it built through words, actions, or both?

    o   How can I continue to strengthen my trust in my Dominant? What small steps can I take to build even deeper trust?

    o   When I feel vulnerable or unsure, how do I remind myself of my trust in my Dominant? How does it help me to continue surrendering?

Closing Reflection:

Trust is the foundation of any strong D/s dynamic. It allows you to surrender, explore, and grow within the safety of your relationship. By trusting your Dominant, you create a space where vulnerability is met with care and respect, and both partners can thrive emotionally and physically. Trust isn't given blindly—it's built, reaffirmed, and deepened over time through actions, communication, and mutual respect. Through trust, submission becomes an act of surrender and a powerful tool for connection and growth.

Personal Reflections:

Understanding the Desire to Submit

Meditation:

Find a quiet and comfortable space to sit or lie down. Close your eyes and take a few deep breaths, letting go of distractions. Feel a sense of calmness filling your body; with each exhale, release any tension or lingering thoughts.

Now, focus on the desire to submit. Reflect on why submission excites and fulfills you. What is it about surrendering control that resonates with you on a deep level? Is it the trust, the intimacy, the release of pressure, or something else entirely? Think about how submission aligns with your desires and what it offers you regarding emotional, physical, and psychological fulfillment.

Visualize what submission means to you. How does it feel to let go of control and allow your Dominant to take charge? What emotions arise when you embrace your submissive role? Consider the deeper needs that submission fulfills and how they shape your connection with your Dominant.

Affirmation:
I embrace my desire to submit as a path to deeper connection, fulfillment, and growth. Through submission, I experience release, trust, and empowerment.

- **Practices in Action**:

Activity 1: Exploring the Roots of Your Submission
Take some time to reflect on your journey to understand your need for submission. What experiences or feelings first led you to embrace this role? Was it an intuitive feeling, or did it evolve? Share these insights with your Dominant. Let them understand the origins of your desire to submit and what it means to you on a deeper level.

Tip: Be open and vulnerable in this practice. Understanding your submission's roots helps you and your Dominant connect more profoundly and honor your dynamic more fully.

Activity 2: Sharing Your Desires
Share your deepest desires with your Dominant. These may be fantasies, emotional needs, or specific aspects of submission that excite you. Allow yourself to be open, honest, and vulnerable as you express what you crave from the dynamic.

Tip: This is an opportunity to communicate openly without fear of judgment. Being clear about your desires allows your Dominant to support you in fulfilling them while deepening trust and intimacy.

Activity 3: Understanding Submission Through Reflection
After a scene or experience that you've submitted, reflect on how it made you feel. How did it satisfy the more profound needs you have for submission? Were there moments when you felt truly connected and fulfilled? Consider what aspects of the experience brought you the most joy or satisfaction.

Tip: Journaling or discussing these reflections with your Dominant will help clarify your desires and allow you to fine-tune your dynamic based on mutual understanding.

- **Journaling Prompts**:

  o   What is it about submission that excites me? How does it fulfill me emotionally, physically, and mentally?

  o   How do I feel when I allow myself to embrace submission fully? What does it offer me in terms of release or connection?

  o   What deeper needs or desires does submission satisfy for me?

  o   How has my understanding of my need for submission shaped my relationship with my Dominant?

  o   < UNK> How can I communicate my desires more clearly to my Dominant, and how does that enhance our connection?

Closing Reflection:

Understanding the desire to submit is an essential part of the submissive journey. It helps you connect more deeply with yourself and your Dominant. Acknowledging the emotional, physical, and psychological fulfillment submission offers opens up a space for growth, trust, and mutual respect within your dynamic. Submission isn't just about the act itself—it's about the deeper emotional and relational needs it satisfies for you and your Dominant. Understanding these desires creates a more empowered and connected dynamic that fosters true intimacy.

Personal Reflections:

The Beauty of Surrender

Meditation:

Find a quiet space and sit comfortably, allowing your body to relax. Take a few deep breaths to center yourself, inhaling calmness and exhaling any tension or stress.

Now, visualize yourself in a scene where you completely surrender to your Dominant's guidance. Picture the moment you let go of control and trust them wholly to take the lead. How does it feel to release your grip and allow yourself to be guided? Is there a sense of peace, liberation, or vulnerability in this act of surrender? Allow yourself to experience the emotions that arise as you embrace this state of surrender.

Reflect on the trust that comes with surrender. What does it feel like to let go, to be held in the hands of someone who respects and cares for you? Consider the power in the vulnerability of surrender and how it opens up space for deeper intimacy and connection between you and your Dominant.

Affirmation:
I surrender with trust and openness, embracing the beauty of being guided. Through surrender, I experience freedom, connection, and growth.

- **Practices in Action**:

  Activity 1: Embracing a New Scene Focused on Surrender
  Engage in a scene where surrender is central. This could involve a role-play scenario where you allow your Dominant to take control in ways you haven't explored before. Focus on letting go of any lingering control or fear, and immerse yourself in the experience of being fully guided.

  Tip: Let go of expectations and truly surrender to the moment. Trust that your Dominant is there to guide you safely and with care.

  Activity 2: Communicating Your Experience of Surrender
  After the scene, reflect on how it felt to surrender. How did it affect your emotional and physical state? Was there a release of tension or a sense of peace in giving up control? Share these feelings with your Dominant, letting them know how the experience influenced you.

  Tip: Open communication after a scene is essential. This allows you to understand how surrender affected you and what can be improved or further explored.

  Activity 3: Exploring Vulnerability in Surrender
  Think about how vulnerability plays a role in the surrender. Explore how it feels to be truly vulnerable and open with your Dominant, whether through emotional expression, physical submission, or mental release. Embrace the discomfort and beauty of vulnerability, knowing that surrender can be a transformative experience.

Tip: Vulnerability can feel uncomfortable, but it's also an opportunity for growth and connection. Approach it with curiosity and openness.

- **Journaling Prompts**:

    o How does it feel to give up control and surrender to my Dominant? What emotions arise in that moment?

    o What does trust look like when I fully surrender? How does it influence my sense of safety and connection?

    o In what ways does surrender enhance my emotional or physical experience during a scene?

    o How can I embrace the vulnerability of surrender without feeling overwhelmed or anxious?

    o What role does surrender play in deepening my relationship with my Dominant? How does it contribute to our trust and intimacy?

Closing Reflection:

Surrender is a powerful and beautiful part of the submissive journey. It is an act of trust, vulnerability, and emotional release. By embracing surrender, you open yourself to a deeper connection with your Dominant, allowing for greater intimacy and mutual respect. Surrender isn't about weakness—it's about strength in vulnerability, trust in your partner, and the willingness to explore new depths of your dynamic. You invite both emotional and physical growth through surrender, enhancing your connection and fostering a profound sense of unity with your Dominant.

Personal Reflections:

Boundaries and Personal Empowerment

Meditation:

Find a comfortable, quiet space to relax in. Close your eyes and take several deep breaths, allowing your body to settle into the present moment. With each inhale, feel calm, exhale, and release any tension.

Now, focus on your boundaries. Visualize your boundaries as a protective yet flexible structure that keeps you safe while allowing for growth and exploration. Reflect on what your boundaries mean to you and how they empower you. Consider how your ability to communicate these boundaries fosters a sense of personal control, even within submission.

Allow yourself to feel the strength in setting limits. How do your boundaries support your emotional, physical, and mental well-being? Visualize yourself clearly expressing these boundaries to your Dominant, and notice how this communication empowers you within the dynamic.

Affirmation:
My boundaries are my strength. I honor and communicate them clearly, knowing they protect and empower me within my submission.

- **Practices in Action**:

    Activity 1: Communicating a Boundary
    Choose a moment during your day to communicate a boundary with your Dominant. This could be as simple as saying "no" to something that doesn't feel right or expressing a limit you want respected during a scene. Practice stating your boundaries clearly and without hesitation, knowing you are empowering yourself.

    Tip: Use "I" statements when communicating your boundaries (e.g., "I feel uncomfortable with..."). This keeps the conversation focused on your feelings and needs, which promotes healthy communication.

    Activity 2: Reflecting on Boundaries During a Scene
    Before beginning a scene, reflect on the boundaries you need to set in that moment. Whether physical, emotional, or mental, affirming your limits ensures you enter the scene with confidence and clarity. Afterward, reflect on how honoring those boundaries made you feel empowered or more connected to your Dominant.

    Tip: Respecting your boundaries enhances trust in the dynamic. Revisit moments during the scene where you felt your limits were respected and appreciate the empowerment from this respect.

Activity 3: Exploring Empowerment Through Boundary Setting
Reflect on how setting and maintaining your boundaries empowers you within and outside the dynamic. How does your submission become more robust when you know your limits are respected? Expressing your boundaries leads to greater self-awareness, confidence, and emotional well-being.

Tip: When you honor your boundaries, it becomes easier to give more fully, knowing that your emotional and physical safety is prioritized. This trust in yourself and your Dominant deepens your dynamic.

- **Journaling Prompts**:

    o   How do my boundaries empower me within the context of submission?

    o   In what ways do my boundaries reflect my emotional, physical, and mental well-being?

    o   How can I clearly communicate my limits to ensure my needs are met?

    o   What feelings arise when I assert my boundaries? How do these feelings strengthen my submission?

    o   How does honoring my boundaries contribute to my growth and sense of self within the dynamic?

Closing Reflection:

Boundaries are vital to personal empowerment within any relationship, especially in a power exchange dynamic. They provide a foundation of trust and safety, allowing both partners to explore more profound levels of connection and vulnerability. By communicating your boundaries clearly and confidently, you assert your emotional and physical autonomy, which strengthens the submissive role. Your boundaries are not just limits—they are sources of strength, resilience, and self-respect. Honoring them within the dynamic nurtures a healthy balance where both partners can grow, explore, and thrive together.

Personal Reflections:

Finding Strength in Obedience

Meditation:

Find a quiet space where you can relax. Close your eyes and take a few deep breaths, grounding yourself in the present moment. With each inhale, feel a wave of calmness spread throughout your body, and exhale, release any tension or distractions.

Now, reflect on obedience as an act of strength and trust. Visualize yourself surrendering to your Dominant's guidance, fully trusting them to lead you without hesitation. How does it feel to place your trust in someone else's decisions?

Consider how obedience requires strength—not weakness, but the power to let go, follow, and trust. Reflect on how this obedience strengthens your emotional connection with your Dominant, creating a deeper bond of respect and understanding. Allow yourself to feel empowered in surrender, knowing your submission is a conscious and powerful choice.

Affirmation:
Obedience is an act of strength. I trust my dominance and honor obedience's strength to our connection.

- **Practices in Action**:

  Activity 1: Surrendering to a Task Without Question
  Allow your Dominant to lead you through a task without questioning your decision. Whether it's a simple chore, a scene, or an emotional request, focus on surrendering to the experience without resistance. Notice how it feels to be guided by your Dominant and how this obedience builds trust and deepens your connection.

  Tip: Embrace the task thoroughly and focus on the emotions that arise during the process. How does it feel to be led, and how does that strengthen your bond with your Dominant?

  Activity 2: Obedience as Trust in Action
  Reflect on how obedience is not just an action but a reflection of your trust. Practice submitting to your Dominant's desires and instructions during play or daily life, trusting that they have your best interests at heart. Notice how your emotional connection grows through this act of trust.

  Tip: When you obey, you reinforce your Dominant's role and deepen the trust that forms the foundation of your dynamic. Celebrate the strength it takes to trust them fully.

Activity 3: Exploring the Emotional Impact of Obedience

After a task or scene where you've obeyed without hesitation, reflect on how it made you feel emotionally. Did you feel closer to your Dominant? Did obedience bring up feelings of gratitude or empowerment? Reflect on how obedience helps you cultivate a deeper connection.

Tip: Take note of the emotional shifts after moments of obedience. It can help you better understand the emotional power of surrendering to your Dominant.

- **Journaling Prompts**:

    o   How does obedience make me feel in terms of strength and trust?

    o   What emotions arise when I surrender to my Dominant's guidance?

    o   How does obedience enhance my emotional connection to my Dominant?

    o   What strength do I find in obedience, and how does it empower me?

    o   How can I further embrace the power of obedience in my submission?

Closing Reflection:

Obedience is often misunderstood as a sign of weakness, but it is a profound act of strength and trust. Through obedience, you are choosing to place your trust in your Dominant, strengthening your emotional connection and deepening your bond. This act of surrender allows for growth, not only in the dynamic but also in your strength as a submissive. Embrace the power of obedience as it fosters a deeper level of trust, connection, and intimacy within your relationship.

Personal Reflections:

The Balance of Power in Submission

Meditation:

Find a quiet and comfortable space. Close your eyes and take a few deep breaths, allowing your body to relax with each inhale. As you breathe in, feel a sense of calmness filling you; as you breathe out, release any tension you may be holding.

Now, focus on balancing your submission and your Dominant's power. Imagine a dynamic of give and take, where energy flows between you harmoniously. Reflect on how your submission allows your Dominant to lead, but also how your ability to surrender grants them the responsibility to care for and nurture you.

Visualize this balance as a dance between you and your Dominant. Your submission does not diminish you; it enhances your connection, allowing them to guide you with authority and love. Notice how both of you influence this balance, creating a space where power is shared, not taken, and where care and trust are at the forefront.

Affirmation:
My submission and my Dominant's power create a balanced, caring dynamic. We share power, and through it, we deepen our connection.

- **Practices in Action**:

Activity 1: Discussing the Balance of Power
Discuss openly with your Dominant about how power is shared in your dynamic. Share your thoughts on how both of you contribute to the balance of power and care. Reflect on how your submission enhances their energy and how their power supports your submission.

Tip: Approach the conversation with openness and curiosity. Both partners should feel heard and respected as you explore how power is balanced in your relationship.

Activity 2: Engaging in a Balanced Power Exchange
During a scene or experience, consciously focus on the balance of power between you and your Dominant. Please consider how you feel when you submit and how your Dominant exercises their power carefully. Notice how the dynamic shifts when you are mindful of the balance between control and care.

Tip: Take mental notes of how the exchange feels in real-time. Reflect on whether you feel supported, empowered, and respected and how this balance enhances your experience.

Activity 3: Revisiting the Power Dynamics in Everyday Life
After a scene or intense moment, revisit the balance of power in your everyday interactions. How do you both share power outside of the play space? Does your Dominant's guidance extend into moments of vulnerability or decision-making in your daily life? Reflect on how this balance carries over into your relationship beyond BDSM activities.

Tip: Incorporate power-sharing moments in your daily routines, such as decision-making or discussing emotional needs. This will strengthen the foundation of your dynamic.

- **Journaling Prompts**:

    o   How do I feel when power is shared in my dynamic?

    o   How does my submission contribute to the power dynamics within our relationship?

    o   What role does care play in the balance of power between us?

    o   How does my Dominant's care for me influence the power exchange?

    o   How do I experience power when I am fully in my submission?

Closing Reflection:

The balance of power in submission is a delicate and dynamic process. It is not about one partner holding all the power but about how the energy flow is shared and respected. Through submission, you are allowing your Dominant to guide you, but they are also responsible for caring for and nurturing you. When power is balanced with care, both partners can thrive, and your connection deepens. This balance enhances trust, respect, and intimacy, creating a space where both submission and power coexist harmoniously.

Personal Reflections:

Embracing the Emotional Depth of Submission

Meditation:

Find a comfortable space and close your eyes. Take a deep breath, exhaling to release any tension in your body. Let your mind relax as you focus on the emotional layers beneath your submission.

Now, reflect on the emotional depth of submission. What emotions arise when you surrender, and how do they influence your connection with your Dominant? Imagine submission as well, with each act of surrender allowing you to uncover deeper layers of emotion. Do you feel vulnerability, trust, fear, or peace? Consider how these emotions shift your experience of submission and how they allow for greater intimacy.

Affirmation:

My submission allows me to explore the depths of my emotions. I embrace vulnerability and trust, knowing that each emotional layer brings us closer together.

- **Practices in Action**:

Activity 1: Engaging in an Emotional Conversation
Take time to have an open and honest conversation with your Dominant about your emotional needs. Share how submission impacts your emotional state, and express any feelings that arise during moments of surrender. This will help deepen your understanding of your emotional connection and allow your Dominant to support you more effectively.

Tip: Approach the conversation honestly and openly, creating a space where both partners can express their feelings without judgment.

Activity 2: Exploring Emotional Vulnerability in Submission
During a scene, allow yourself to become fully immersed in the emotions of submission. Focus on the feelings of trust, vulnerability, or peace that arise as you surrender control. Notice how these emotions affect your physical experience and connection with your Dominant.

Tip: Pay attention to the emotions that surface in the moment, and try to name them. This will help you process them more clearly and share them with your Dominant.

Activity 3: Emotional Check-In After a Scene
After a scene, take time to check in with your emotional state. Share with your Dominant any emotions that emerged during the experience, both positive and challenging. This will help you reflect on how emotional depth plays a role in your submission and how your Dominant can help guide you through those emotions.

Tip: Be open to processing emotional vulnerability's highs and lows. This dialogue strengthens your bond and helps you understand each other better.

- **Journaling Prompts**:

    o   What emotions arise for me when I submit?

    o   How does surrendering control make me feel on an emotional level?

    o   What insights have I gained about my emotional needs through submission?

    o   How does my Dominant support my emotional journey in submission?

    o   How can I deepen my emotional connection with my Dominant through submission?

Closing Reflection:

Submission is not just a physical act but a profoundly emotional experience. The emotional depth that comes with submission can reveal new aspects of yourself, from vulnerability and trust to peace and clarity. Embracing this emotional journey opens the door to greater intimacy and connection with your Dominant. Submission allows you to explore the depths of your desires and the layers of your emotions, creating a dynamic that is both fulfilling and transformative. When submission is approached with emotional openness, it becomes a powerful tool for self-discovery and deepened connection.

Personal Reflections:

Patience and Trusting the Process

Meditation:

Find a quiet, comfortable space and close your eyes. Take a deep breath, and as you exhale, let go of any tension you may be holding. Allow your body to relax as you settle into the present moment.

Now, picture your submission as a journey that unfolds over time. Imagine each step of this journey as a building block, each experience adding depth to your connection and understanding. As you picture this unfolding, reflect on the process rather than the immediate results. How does it feel to trust that the journey, with all its highs and lows, will lead to more significant growth? Notice how patience plays a key role, allowing you to experience submission without rushing and embrace the process as it is.

Affirmation:
I trust in the submission process. I allow myself to grow at my own pace, embracing each step as a valuable part of my journey.

- **Practices in Action**:

   Activity 1: Engaging in a Slow and Deliberate Scene
   Create a scene where the pace is intentionally slow and deliberate. Take your time with each action, each word, and each touch. As the submissive, surrender to the slow rhythm and fully allow yourself to experience each moment. Focus on the sensations that arise, appreciating the slow unfolding of the dynamic.

   Tip: Use this time to practice patience and trust in the process. Allow yourself to be present without rushing toward an outcome.

   Activity 2: Reflecting on the Journey of Submission
   Take time to reflect on the overall journey of your submission. How have you grown through patience and time? What has unfolded throughout your relationship or your submission that may have felt rushed if you hadn't taken your time? Share your thoughts with your Dominant, and discuss how the slow process has shaped your submission.

   Tip: Think about where you started and how far you've come. This reflection helps you appreciate the process and the lessons learned along the way.

   Activity 3: Fostering Patience During Moments of Challenge
   During moments of challenge or discomfort in a scene, practice patience by focusing on your breath and reminding yourself that this is part of the process. Trust that each moment of discomfort can lead to deeper understanding and growth. Embrace the experience as a step in your journey; patience is vital to navigating it.

Tip: Instead of rushing to escape discomfort, focus on surrendering to it, trusting that the journey will ultimately bring you closer to your desires and growth.

- **Journaling Prompts**:

  o How does patience change the way I experience submission?

  o In what ways has the slow unfolding of my submission led to a deeper understanding?

  o What challenges have I faced that required patience, and how have they strengthened my submission?

  o How can I practice more patience in my submission, both in and out of scenes?

  o What do I trust about the submission process, and how does that trust affect my dynamic?

Closing Reflection:

Submission is not always about instant gratification or immediate results; it is a journey that takes time. Patience allows you to deepen your submission and to experience each moment fully without rushing toward the next. Trusting the process means surrendering to the unfolding of your relationship and the dynamic, knowing that each step, even the challenging ones, leads to growth. Through patience, you allow both yourself and your Dominant to cultivate a deeper, more meaningful connection, one that is built over time and nurtured with care.

Personal Reflections:

Receiving Guidance and Growth

Meditation:

Find a comfortable place to sit or lie down without distraction. Close your eyes and take a deep breath, releasing tension with each exhale. Allow your body to relax, becoming fully present in the moment.

Now, visualize your Dominant's guidance as a steady and supportive presence. See how their wisdom, care, and leadership help foster your growth within your submission and all areas of your life. As you reflect on this, consider how their guidance shapes you into a stronger, more self-aware person. Imagine your growth as a blossoming flower, nurtured by their direction, and feel how their presence empowers you to explore and reach new heights.

Affirmation:
I am open to receiving guidance, and I trust that my Dominant's direction fosters my personal growth.

- **Practices in Action**:

Activity 1: Asking for Advice or Support
Reach out to your Dominant for advice or support in a new area of your life—this could be related to a personal goal, career, or emotional well-being. Share openly with them and allow their guidance to help you navigate this new challenge. As the submissive, trust in their wisdom and lean into their leadership, knowing that their support will help you grow.

Tip: Be specific about the area in which you need guidance. This helps your Dominant provide focused and meaningful advice.

Activity 2: Reflecting on Past Guidance
Take time to reflect on the guidance your Dominant has given you in the past. How has their leadership contributed to your growth in both small and significant ways? Write specific examples of their support, and consider how those moments have shaped your personal development.

Tip: Look at the areas where you have felt the most growth. Reflect on how your Dominant's guidance influenced that process and what it taught you about yourself.

Activity 3: Embracing Growth in Other Areas of Your Life
Submit to a new challenge outside of your dynamic that requires you to step up and grow. This could be something personal, professional, or spiritual. As you work through this challenge, remember how your Dominant's guidance has prepared you to face it. Reflect on how the skills you've learned from submission can translate into other areas of your life.

Tip: Embrace this activity to show your Dominant how their guidance has empowered you to expand and grow in various aspects of your life.

- **Journaling Prompts**:

  - How has my Dominant's guidance contributed to my growth in specific areas of my life?

  - What aspects of my life do I wish to seek more guidance, and how can I be open to receiving it?

  - In what ways has submission empowered me to grow as an individual, both within and outside the dynamic?

  - How do I feel when I receive guidance from my Dominant?

  - What have I learned about myself through receiving support and direction?

Closing Reflection:

Receiving guidance is an essential part of submission. Through the wisdom and care of your Dominant, you can grow emotionally, mentally, and even spiritually. Their leadership fosters your transformation, helping you become the best version of yourself. Submission isn't just about surrender; it's about embracing the growth that comes from trusting and learning from your Dominant's guidance. When you open yourself to their support, you allow your dynamic to flourish and grow, making each step of the journey more meaningful and empowering.

Personal Reflections:

The Role of Ritual in Submission

Meditation:

Find a quiet and comfortable space. Close your eyes and take a few deep, slow breaths, allowing your body to relax with each exhale. Focus on the present moment, and release any tension you may be holding.

Now, visualize a ritual that reinforces your bond with your Dominant. Imagine the details—perhaps it's the sound of their voice as they issue an instruction or the sensation of their touch as they guide you through a sacred moment of submission. Picture the emotions that arise as you fully surrender to this ritual, feeling a deep connection, trust, and respect.

Reflect on how rituals play an important role in reinforcing your submission. How do these repeated actions or words deepen the emotional bond between you and your Dominant? What is it about the ritual that submits feel more sacred and meaningful?

Affirmation:
Through ritual, I strengthen my connection with my Dominant, reaffirming my submission and trust.

- **Practices in Action**:

  Activity 1: Participating in a Submission Ritual
  Choose a ritual, either one you already practice or one you create that reaffirms your submission. This could be something as simple as an affirmation exchange, a physical gesture like kneeling, or something more elaborate like a collaring ceremony. Focus on the emotions you experience during the ritual, and allow yourself to surrender to the act entirely.

  Tip: Make the ritual personal and meaningful to your dynamic. It can be a small act or a more significant, symbolic gesture. What matters is the intention behind it.

  Activity 2: Affirmation Exchange
  Share affirmations with your Dominant, expressing your submission and affirming your trust. This can be a verbal exchange, a written note, or a physical act that shows your submission. Reaffirming your submission through words or actions can strengthen the emotional foundation of your dynamic.

  Tip: Use affirmations that resonate with both of you and reflect your shared values within the relationship. These can be tailored to reinforce your connection.

Activity 3: Reflecting on Ritual's Impact
After participating in a ritual or affirmation exchange, reflect on how it impacted your connection with your Dominant. How did it affect your sense of trust and vulnerability? How did the ritual enhance your submission and deepen your emotional bond? Write down your thoughts and reflect on the significance of ritual in your relationship.

Tip: Be open to the emotional shifts that rituals can bring. They can help you connect more deeply with your Dominant, fostering trust and intimacy.

- **Journaling Prompts**:

    o What role do rituals play in deepening my submission?

    o How does a ritual help me feel more connected to my Dominant?

    o What are the emotions I experience during a submission ritual?

    o How can I create new rituals that strengthen my submission?

    o In what ways do rituals help me maintain trust and respect in the dynamic?

Closing Reflection:

Rituals are potent tools in submission, reinforcing trust, respect, and the emotional bond between you and your Dominant. Whether simple or elaborate, rituals allow you to step deeper into your submission, creating a sense of security and connection. Through these practices, you honor your role and the strength of your bond. Rituals help to affirm your submission, making the relationship more sacred and meaningful and strengthening the trust and intimacy you share.

Personal Reflections:

Releasing Control to Embrace Freedom

Meditation:

Find a quiet space where you can sit or lie comfortably. Close your eyes and take deep, grounding breaths. Inhale deeply, fill your lungs with calm energy, and exhale slowly, releasing any tension or worry.

Now, focus on the concept of releasing control. Visualize yourself in a moment where you surrender all power to your Dominant, trusting them to guide you completely. Notice how it feels—perhaps there is initial resistance, fear, and a growing sense of freedom as you let go. Reflect on how this surrender opens up new emotional and mental space, allowing you to embrace the freedom from trusting and relinquishing control.

Think about how the absence of control allows you to experience the moment fully, free from the need to manage or direct. What does true freedom feel like for you in the context of submission?

Affirmation:
I release control to embrace the freedom that comes from trust and surrender. In letting go, I discover a new strength.

- **Practices in Action**:

  Activity 1: Letting Go of Control
  Choose an activity where you can fully release control to your Dominant. It could be a simple task, such as letting them guide you through a physical activity, or something more emotional, like allowing them to make decisions for you in a situation where you usually have a say. Let go of the need to manage the situation and fully surrender to their leadership.

  Tip: If you feel resistance, acknowledge it but continue to breathe deeply and trust the process. Release your need to control the situation and allow yourself to experience the freedom of surrender.

  Activity 2: Surrendering to Full Control
  Engage in a scene or activity where your Dominant takes complete control. Allow them to guide you through every step, whether physical or mental. Trust that they will care for you and your well-being throughout the experience. Focus on the feeling of freedom that comes from surrendering completely.

  Tip: Pay attention to how you feel in total surrender. What thoughts or emotions arise when you stop trying to control the experience?

Activity 3: Reflecting on Freedom Through Surrender
After letting go of control, reflect on how the experience felt. How did surrendering create emotional space for you? Did you feel a sense of freedom or lightness? Journal about how relinquishing control made you think and how it shifted your perspective on your submission.

Tip: Remember that true freedom often comes from vulnerability. Embrace the feelings that arise, knowing they are part of your growth and deepening connection.

- **Journaling Prompts**:

  o How does releasing control in submission allow me to feel more free?

  o What emotions arise when I let go of control?

  o In what ways does relinquishing control deepen my connection with my Dominant?

  o How can I embrace the freedom of trusting my Dominant to lead?

  o What lessons have I learned from surrendering control in our dynamic?

Closing Reflection:

Surrendering control is an act of trust and empowerment, not weakness. It allows you to experience freedom in ways often impossible when you hold on to control. Through submission, you discover that freedom is found not in exerting power but in releasing it. In this act of surrender, you find peace, security, and a deeper connection with your Dominant. By letting go, you create space for the relationship to grow and evolve, unlocking new layers of emotional depth and freedom.

Personal Reflections:

Exploring the Connection Between Pain and Pleasure

Meditation:

Find a comfortable space to sit or lie down. Close your eyes and take several deep, calming breaths. Inhale deeply through your nose, filling your lungs with peaceful energy, and exhale slowly, releasing any tension from your body.

Focus your attention on the sensations of pain and pleasure. Visualize these sensations as two different energies—one sharp, intense, and perhaps difficult to endure, and the other warm, soothing, and pleasurable. Picture how they interact with one another, how they blend and shift as one. Notice how pain can sharpen your awareness, while pleasure can soothe and release.

Reflect on how these sensations coexist and how one can enhance the other. Explore the idea that through contrast, both pain and pleasure become more intense and vivid, creating a unique experience. How do these sensations affect your emotional state, and how can you allow yourself to experience both with trust and openness fully?

Affirmation:
I embrace the complexity of pain and pleasure, knowing that both contribute to my growth and connection with my Dominant.

- **Practices in Action**:

   Activity 1: Exploring Pain and Pleasure
   Engage in a scene where pain and pleasure are deliberately interwoven. This could involve a controlled experience where your Dominant uses sensation play—such as impact play, temperature play, or other techniques—allowing you to experience the interplay of pain and pleasure. Focus on staying present and letting yourself experience both without judgment.

   Tip: Allow yourself to feel each sensation as it comes. If you're feeling discomfort, try focusing on the pleasure that comes alongside it, allowing it to blend in a way that deepens your experience.

   Activity 2: Boundaries in Pain and Pleasure
   Discuss your limits and comfort zones with your Dominant before beginning. Be clear about the level of intensity you're comfortable with, and ensure that both of you are aligned on what will happen during the scene. Remember that boundaries are essential to maintaining a safe space for exploration.

   Tip: As you experience pain and pleasure, check in with yourself and your Dominant. Is the experience still within your boundaries? How does each sensation feel, and can you differentiate between discomfort and actual pain?

Activity 3: Reflecting on the Emotional Impact
After the scene, reflect on how the combination of pain and pleasure affected you emotionally. Did the experience bring new feelings or insights about yourself, your submission, or your relationship with your Dominant? Journal about your thoughts, emotions, and any discoveries.

Tip: Be gentle with yourself as you reflect. The connection between pain and pleasure can stir deep emotions, and it's important to honor those feelings as part of your journey.

- **Journaling Prompts**:

    o How did the mixture of pain and pleasure affect my emotional experience?

    o In what ways did the contrast between pain and pleasure heighten my awareness and connection with my Dominant?

    o How did the experience deepen my understanding of my limits and desires?

    o What emotional or physical responses did I notice when pain and pleasure were intertwined?

    o How does exploring pain and pleasure in this way enhance my sense of vulnerability and trust with my Dominant?

Closing Reflection:

Exploring pain and pleasure is a profoundly personal experience that can lead to profound emotional insights. As you explore the connection between the two, you may discover new depths of intimacy, vulnerability, and trust in your submission. Pain and pleasure are not opposites; they can work together, enhancing each other and creating a richer, more intense experience. Through mindful exploration, you learn to embrace the complexity of your emotions and submission, allowing both to contribute to your personal growth and deepen your relationship.

Personal Reflections:

Learning to Let Go of Guilt

Meditation:
Find a quiet and comfortable space. Close your eyes and take a few slow, deep breaths, letting your body relax with each exhale. Allow your mind to focus on releasing any tension or self-judgment.

Reflect on guilt—what does it feel like, and how does it affect your emotional and mental state? Imagine yourself holding onto guilt as a heavy burden, weighing you down. With each breath, visualize that burden lightening, the guilt dissolving, leaving you with peace and self-acceptance.

Picture yourself fully embracing the idea of forgiveness for yourself and others. Visualize your Dominant extending compassion and understanding towards you, allowing you to feel safe in their care. Reflect on the importance of releasing guilt and recognizing that mistakes are growth opportunities, not reasons for shame.

Affirmation:
I release guilt and embrace forgiveness. I trust in my Dominant's care and the power of self-acceptance.

- **Practices in Action**:

  Activity 1: Sharing a Past Mistake
  Open up to your Dominant about a past mistake or misstep for which you still feel guilt. This could be related to your submission or outside the dynamic. Speak openly and without fear of judgment, allowing yourself to be vulnerable in sharing. Allow your Dominant to listen with understanding and provide forgiveness, creating space for healing.

  Tip: Approach this conversation with openness and honesty. If you find it difficult to share, start by acknowledging any fear or shame that may arise. Remember that forgiveness is a tool for growth, not a punishment.

  Activity 2: Receiving Forgiveness
  Once you've shared your past mistakes, let yourself truly experience the power of forgiveness. Allow your Dominant to express their care, understanding, and support. Embrace the feeling of being forgiven and the relief that comes with it. Notice how this forgiveness deepens your connection and allows you to move forward with more trust and peace.

  Tip: Focus on how forgiveness feels from your Dominant and yourself. Notice the emotional release when you accept forgiveness and how this opens up space for growth and a deeper bond.

Activity 3: Letting Go of Self-Judgment

After receiving forgiveness, reflect on how your guilt has shaped your submission. How does it feel to let go of this weight? How does forgiving yourself contribute to your emotional well-being and the strength of your submission? Allow yourself to embrace self-acceptance and the knowledge that mistakes are part of the journey, not barriers.

Tip: Be kind to yourself as you process these feelings. Self-compassion is a crucial part of your submission, and it's essential to recognize that mistakes don't diminish your worth or your place within the dynamic.

- **Journaling Prompts**:

    o How did sharing a past mistake with my Dominant feel?

    o What did I learn about myself by receiving forgiveness?

    o In what ways does releasing guilt make room for deeper trust and connection with my Dominant?

    o How does forgiving myself contribute to my emotional growth and my submission?

    o What does self-acceptance look like in my submission, and how can I continue to practice it?

Closing Reflection:

Letting go of guilt is an act of profound self-compassion and growth. By releasing the weight of past mistakes, you make space for healing and deeper trust in your Dominant and yourself. Forgiveness is a gift given by others and one you give yourself. As you embrace self-acceptance, you strengthen your emotional connection, deepening your submission and relationship. Remember, submission is not about perfection but vulnerability, growth, and the courage to face your mistakes with grace and humility.

Personal Reflections:

The Intimacy of Service

Meditation:

Find a quiet, comfortable space to sit and relax. Close your eyes, take a few deep breaths, and center yourself in the present moment. With each inhale, feel calm, exhale, and release any tension.

Focus on the act of service as a manifestation of your devotion to your Dominant. Visualize performing acts of service with intention, seeing each task as a way to express your care, respect, and commitment to them. Picture yourself offering this service, not from a place of obligation but from a deep emotional connection that strengthens your bond.

Reflect on how service in your submissive role creates intimacy between you and your Dominant. How do the small gestures and thoughtful acts of service enhance the emotional and spiritual connection? Notice the satisfaction that arises within you as you serve and how it deepens your relationship.

Affirmation:
My service is an expression of my devotion. By serving my Dominant, I strengthen our bond and deepen our emotional connection.

- **Practices in Action**:

  Activity 1: Performing a Small Service
  Choose a small act of service to perform for your Dominant. It could be something as simple as preparing a meal, running an errand, or helping them with a task that holds significance in your dynamic. Focus on the intention behind your service—doing it with love, respect, and attentiveness. Notice how this act makes you feel as you give of yourself to your Dominant.

  Tip: Try to stay present with your emotions as you perform the service. Notice any feelings that arise—gratitude, love, devotion—and use them to fuel the sincerity of your actions.

  Activity 2: A Gesture of Devotion
  Consider a ritual or gesture of devotion that you can offer to your Dominant. This could be a daily ritual, a handwritten note, or a specific way you show affection through service. The act itself is less important than the intention and the emotional energy behind it. Let it be something meaningful that allows you to express your commitment to your Dominant.

  Tip: Focus on the emotional connection in the gesture. Notice how it feels to serve from a place of genuine care and how that deepens your connection.

Activity 3: Reflecting on the Intimacy of Service
After performing an act of service, please take a moment to reflect on how it made you feel. Did you feel closer to your Dominant? Did the act of service create a sense of fulfillment or joy? Consider how your role as a submissive in this act of service fosters intimacy and strengthens your relationship.

Tip: Keep a journal of these reflections, noting how each act of service deepens your connection. Look for patterns in how service affects your emotional bond and how your Dominant responds to your actions.

- **Journaling Prompts**:

    o   How does performing acts of service for my Dominant make me feel?

    o   What emotions arise when I serve with devotion?

    o   How does service help me feel more connected to my Dominant?

    o   In what ways does my service deepen the intimacy between us?

    o   How can I be more intentional in my acts of service to my Dominant?

Closing Reflection:

Service is an intimate and powerful way to express your submission and devotion. Through service, you contribute to the dynamic and deepen the emotional bond with your Dominant. The act of service becomes a way to connect on a profound level, reinforcing trust, respect, and affection. By offering your service with intention and care, you create an environment where intimacy flourishes and strengthens the connection between you and your Dominant.

Personal Reflections:

The Role of Silence in Submission

Meditation:

Find a quiet space where you can sit comfortably and close your eyes. Take several deep breaths, inhaling calm and exhaling any tension. With each breath, allow yourself to relax and center in the present moment.

Focus on the power of silence in your submission. Reflect on how silence—within a scene or between you and your Dominant—can hold a profound meaning. What does silence feel like in your submission? Does it deepen your focus, making you feel more attuned to your Dominant's presence and direction? Notice how silence can create a sacred space for connection, where words are unnecessary, and trust and understanding flow freely between you.

Imagine yourself in a moment of stillness, fully present in your submission, the quiet strengthening your surrender. Reflect on how silence enhances your experience and deepens your relationship.

Affirmation:
In silence, I find clarity and connection. Through silence, my submission deepens, and my bond with my Dominant grows stronger.

- **Practices in Action**:

Activity 1: A Silent Scene
Engage in a scene where silence plays a central role. You and your Dominant can communicate through gestures, touch, or eye contact rather than words. Focus on how the silence feels as you surrender to the experience. Let go of any need for verbal affirmation, trusting that the non-verbal cues will guide you.

Tip: During this silent scene, pay close attention to how your body responds. Does the quiet heighten your sensitivity to touch? Does it amplify your emotional connection? Use this silence as a tool to foster more profound submission and trust.

Activity 2: Silent Reflection
Reflect quietly after a scene, allowing space for your emotions to settle. Sit with your thoughts without speaking and observe any feelings or insights that arise. This silent reflection can help you connect more deeply with your submission and your Dominant's role in your journey.

Tip: Use this time to tune into your inner state, recognizing the shifts in your emotions, thoughts, and energy. Silence can often reveal truths that words cannot.

Activity 3: Non-Verbal Communication
In everyday interactions with your Dominant, experiment with communicating without words. This could be as simple as a touch on the arm, a look, or a gesture that conveys your submission. Notice how this non-verbal communication enhances your emotional connection and submission.

Tip: Be mindful of the subtle ways you communicate through silence. Pay attention to how your body language shifts when you're in a submissive state and how your Dominant responds.

- **Journaling Prompts**:

    o   How does silence feel in my submission?

    o   In what ways does silence deepen my connection with my Dominant?

    o   How can I embrace silence as a tool for deepening submission?

    o   What emotions arise when I am silent in my submission?

    o   How does non-verbal communication enhance my role as a submissive?

Closing Reflection:

Silence holds a unique power within the dynamic of submission. It allows for deeper connection, amplifies nonverbal communication, and creates a space for trust and understanding to flourish. By embracing silence, you open yourself to a more profound experience of submission that transcends words and speaks directly to the heart. Silence is not emptiness—a rich, meaningful space where your submission deepens and your bond with your Dominant becomes more profound.

Personal Reflections:

Exploring Your Need for Structure

Meditation:

Find a quiet and comfortable place to sit, taking several deep breaths to center yourself. Inhale deeply, fill your lungs with calm, and exhale slowly, releasing any tension. As you settle into the present moment, focus on the feeling of structure and routine in your life.

Reflect on how structure provides you with comfort and stability. Consider the moments when your Dominant's sense of order and guidance has brought clarity and peace. What does it feel like to submit to a carefully planned routine, knowing it creates a sense of balance and purpose in your dynamic? How does structure allow you to trust more deeply and surrender in a way that fosters growth?

Visualize yourself within the boundaries of a well-structured dynamic, where each action has its place, and you feel both held and free. Allow yourself to feel the security and peace that structure brings as you embrace your submission.

Affirmation:
I find comfort and strength in structure. Under the guidance of my Dominant, I embrace routine to deepen my submission.

- **Practices in Action**:

    Activity 1: Following a Structured Routine
    Have your Dominant create a daily or weekly routine for you to follow. This could include specific tasks, rituals, or moments of reflection. Embrace the routine fully, focusing on how following the structure feels and how it enhances your submission. Please pay attention to the structure's stability and how it deepens your understanding of trust and devotion.

    Tip: While following the routine, notice how your emotional state shifts. Does the structure bring a sense of calm or discipline? Reflect on how it helps you stay present and focused on your submission.

    Activity 2: Creating a Ritual of Submission
    Work with your Dominant to develop a ritual or series of repeated steps, such as a morning ritual, a weekly check-in, or a specific act of service. This can become a cornerstone of your dynamic, reinforcing your submission through regular practice.

    Tip: Allow the ritual to become meaningful over time. Repeating actions can deepen your connection and create a sense of predictability, enhancing your emotional security and submission.

Activity 3: Reflecting on the Role of Structure
After engaging in a structured routine or ritual, reflect on how the experience has affected you. What emotions or insights arose during the process? Did the structure help you feel more connected to your Dominant or more attuned to your submissive role? Reflect on how this structure contributes to the strength and depth of your submission.

Tip: Use this time to tune in to how structure helps you focus your energy and attention, allowing you to submit more deeply and completely.

- **Journaling Prompts**:

  - How does structure help me feel more secure in my submission?

  - In what ways does following a routine enhance my emotional connection with my Dominant?

  - How does the presence of structure help me focus on my role and submission?

  - What aspects of structure bring me the most comfort, and why?

  - How can I embrace structure more fully as part of my submission?

Closing Reflection:

Structure and routine are significant in a submission dynamic, offering stability, clarity, and focus. Allowing your Dominant to guide you through structured experiences creates a space where your submission can flourish and deepen. The structure is not about restriction but providing a framework where trust, growth, and connection can thrive. By embracing routine, you allow yourself to be fully present and devoted to your Dominant, enhancing both your submission and your bond.

Personal Reflections:

Emotional Release Through Submission

Meditation:

Find a quiet, comfortable space where you can sit and relax deeply. Close your eyes, take a deep breath in, and allow yourself to sink into the present moment as you exhale. Feel your body more relaxed, grounded, and open with each breath.

Focus your mind on the concept of emotional release. Visualize it as a cleansing wave that begins at your core, washing away any lingering tension, sadness, or unresolved emotions. Picture yourself surrendering fully to this wave, letting go of anything that no longer serves you.

As you submit to the experience of emotional release, allow the energy to move freely through your body, whether it's a gentle release or a more intense cleansing. Reflect on how your submission opens the door for this release, creating a safe space to feel deeply and let go.

Allow the emotions to rise and flow without judgment. Trust that your Dominant will guide you through this process with care, allowing you to experience the catharsis of embracing vulnerability.

Affirmation:
Through submission, I open myself to emotional release. I trust my Dominant to guide me as I surrender to my feelings, knowing that each release brings me closer to healing and deeper connection.

- **Practices in Action**:

    Activity 1: Surrendering to Emotional Release
    During a scene or a quiet moment with your Dominant, surrender to any emotions that arise. This may include tears, laughter, or a deep feeling of release. Allow your Dominant to guide you through this process, whether through verbal affirmation or physical comfort. The key is to let go and trust that the experience is part of your growth and emotional cleansing.

    Tip: Focus on the physical sensations of release—how your body feels as the tension lifts and your emotions flow. Pay attention to the emotional relief that comes from allowing yourself to express and feel deeply.

    Activity 2: Exploring Emotions in a Safe Space
    Create a safe, open environment with your Dominant to discuss any emotions you've been carrying, whether from the dynamic or outside life. As you share these emotions, allow yourself to be fully vulnerable, trusting that your Dominant will hold space for you.

    Tip: During this practice, focus on the emotional release rather than any specific outcome. The goal is not to control the emotions but to experience them fully and release them with trust and safety.

Activity 3: Reflecting on the Release Process

After an emotional release, reflect on the experience with your dominant. How did it feel to let go of the emotions held within you? What did the process of surrendering to emotional release teach you about yourself? Discuss the power of submission in creating a space for emotional vulnerability and catharsis.

Tip: Share your thoughts on the experience. Did you feel lighter afterward? Did any new emotions arise? How can you use this release as a way to deepen your submission in the future?

- **Journaling Prompts**:

    o   What emotions have I been holding onto that I need to release?

    o   How does my submission create a safe space for emotional release?

    o   In what ways has emotional release through submission deepened my connection with my Dominant?

    o   What is it like to trust my Dominant during an emotional release, knowing they are guiding me with care?

    o   How can I fully surrender to my emotions, allowing myself to feel without fear or shame?

Closing Reflection:

Emotional release is a powerful and cathartic process that deepens your submission and strengthens your connection with your Dominant. Through submission, you allow yourself to express and process emotions in a safe, supportive environment. The act of surrendering to these emotions—whether they are feelings of sadness, joy, or frustration—brings clarity and healing. As you embrace emotional release, you allow yourself to grow emotionally, leading to a more robust, more trusting dynamic with your Dominant. Submission becomes a conduit for healing, emotional exploration, and growth.

Personal Reflections:

The Role of Consent in Your Submission

Meditation:

Find a comfortable space to sit and relax, grounding yourself in the present moment. Close your eyes, take a deep breath, and release any tension you may be holding as you exhale. With each inhale, feel more connected to your inner strength and clarity.

Now, focus inward and reflect on consent's profound role in your submission. Visualize consent as a foundation—strong, steady, and unwavering. See it as the clear communication that holds the dynamic between you and your Dominant in a place of trust and respect.

Allow yourself to reflect on how consent is not just a one-time agreement but an ongoing practice that grows and evolves with your submission. Consider how it empowers you, creating space for trust and mutual respect. Imagine how your willingness to express boundaries and your Dominant's responsiveness to them makes a safe container for your submission to flourish.

Feel the strength from knowing you can communicate and affirm your consent anytime and that your voice matters in the dynamic. Picture how this clarity deepens the connection between you and your Dominant, creating a foundation of understanding that enriches every experience.

Affirmation:

My consent is the foundation of my submission. I honor my ability to communicate my needs and boundaries, trusting that my Dominant will respect and support them.

- **Practices in Action**:

  ### Activity 1: Reaffirming Consent

  Set aside time to have an open conversation with your Dominant about your ongoing consent. Discuss how you feel about the dynamic, what is working, and what may need adjustment. This is an opportunity to express your boundaries, desires, and areas where you want more clarity or communication. Reaffirming consent is an ongoing practice that strengthens your submission.

  Tip: Take this conversation seriously, recognizing that it enhances your connection and trust. Ensure that your Dominant actively listens and responds to your feelings and boundaries. Use this time to express any changes you need, no matter how small.

  ### Activity 2: Establishing Clear Boundaries

  Reflect on any new boundaries that may have arisen or evolved within your submission. Take the time to communicate them clearly to your Dominant, ensuring mutual understanding and respect. Establishing boundaries is a proactive way to reinforce consent and create a safe, supportive space for submission.

Tip: Approach this practice with openness and trust, knowing that boundaries are flexible and can be adjusted over time. Keep the dialogue open so you and your Dominant feel safe and heard.

Activity 3: Consent Check-Ins During a Scene
Check-in during a scene or dynamic interaction to see how you feel about consent. Are you still comfortable with the boundaries you've set? Do you feel respected and supported? If necessary, pause and communicate with your Dominant to ensure the dynamic remains aligned with your consent.

Tip: This check-in doesn't have to interrupt the flow of the scene. It can be as simple as a word or gesture that reassures you both that consent is intact and respected.

- **Journaling Prompts**:

  - What does consent mean to me in my submission?

  - How do I feel when my Dominant honors and respects my boundaries?

  - How has the practice of giving and receiving consent deepened the trust between my Dominant and me?

  - What boundaries do I need to reaffirm or adjust in our dynamic?

  - How can I ensure that consent remains a living, evolving part of my submission?

Closing Reflection:

Consent is the cornerstone of a healthy, dynamic, and fulfilling submission. It ensures that both partners feel safe, respected, and heard. As a submissive, knowing that your consent is honored allows you to surrender to your role fully, trusting that the boundaries you've communicated are respected. This ongoing practice of consent deepens your emotional connection, strengthening the bond of trust between you and your Dominant. Through clear communication and mutual respect, consent becomes not just a set of rules but a living, breathing part of your submission that fosters intimacy, safety, and growth.

Personal Reflections:

Understanding Your Desires Beyond the Scene

Meditation:

Find a quiet space where you can relax and focus inward. Close your eyes and take a deep breath, releasing tension as you exhale. Let your body relax with each breath, and center your mind in the present moment.

Now, bring your awareness to your desires, specifically how they extend beyond the physical realm of BDSM play. Consider how your submission touches different aspects of your life—how it shapes how you interact with your Dominant, others, and yourself. Visualize your desires as a continuous thread that runs through every part of your life, not just during scenes or moments of power exchange.

Reflect on how your submission influences your everyday choices and brings out qualities like attentiveness, devotion, and respect in your interactions. Feel the strength of those desires and how they help you show up authentically, whether in the presence of your dominant or when you're apart. Understand how submission is not just an action but a mindset that affects how you view the world, move through it, and express your love and care.

Affirmation:
My desires go beyond the scene. I carry my submission with me in all areas of my life, allowing it to guide my actions and interactions.

- **Practices in Action**:

    Activity 1: Sharing Desires Outside of Play
    Set aside time to share the desires you experience outside of scenes with your Dominant. These may include aspects of your personality, goals, or how you express your submission daily. This practice allows you to connect more deeply, understanding that submission is not confined to the bedroom—it's a part of who you are.

    Tip: Be open and honest about the ways your desires show up outside of BDSM play. This can lead to a richer connection, as your Dominant may be able to support and nurture these desires in different contexts.

    Activity 2: Integrating Submission into Daily Life
    Take time to explore how submission can influence your everyday actions. This could include small acts of service, attentiveness, or mindfulness. You may incorporate rituals or expressions of submission into your routine, such as serving your Dominant in ways that extend beyond the scene or simply showing them care in small gestures that affirm your devotion.

    Tip: View submission as a holistic practice, not confined to specific moments, but something that permeates your interactions with others and yourself.

Activity 3: Reflecting on the Bigger Picture

After an experience of submission, reflect on how it impacts your life beyond the scene. How do your desires and actions in the scene carry over into your day-to-day life? Are there patterns or behaviors that manifest outside of BDSM play that reflect your submission? Recognizing these moments can deepen your understanding of how your desires guide you in all aspects of life.

Tip: Note any small or large ways your submission extends beyond play and celebrate how it enriches your overall submission experience.

- **Journaling Prompts**:

  - How do my desires as a submissive influence my actions and behaviors outside of play?

  - In what ways do I carry my submission into my everyday interactions?

  - How can I express my devotion and submission even when not in a BDSM context?

  - What are the more profound, non-physical aspects of my submission that I may want to explore further?

  - How does submitting in all areas of my life help me grow?

Closing Reflection:

Submission is not confined to a single moment or scene—it is a powerful thread that weaves through every part of your life. By understanding how your desires extend beyond the physical play, you deepen your connection to your Dominant and yourself. Submission becomes a mindset, a way of living that touches how you approach your relationships, work, and personal growth. As you embrace your submission in all its forms, you allow it to guide you toward a more authentic, fulfilling life.

Personal Reflections:

Embracing Your Role in the Power Exchange

Meditation:

Find a quiet space and take a few deep breaths, allowing your body to relax and your mind to clear. Inhale deeply, and as you exhale, let go of any tension in your body.

Now, bring your awareness to your role within the power exchange. Visualize the dynamic between you and your Dominant, focusing on the power flow and how your submission fits into this more extensive exchange. Imagine the balance between your needs, desires, and boundaries and how they intertwine with your Dominant's needs, desires, and leadership.

Reflect on the trust and responsibility inherent in the exchange. How does submission give you a sense of purpose within the dynamic? Consider how honoring your role allows the Dominant to guide, protect, and nurture you while also allowing you to express your deepest desires and needs. Feel the connection between your submission and the power exchange, knowing that both partners play an integral role in this dance of power and trust.

Affirmation:
I embrace my role in the power exchange. My submission strengthens our dynamic, and we honor and fulfill each other's needs.

- **Practices in Action**:

    Activity 1: Discussing Roles and Needs
    Have an open conversation with your Dominant about your respective roles in the power exchange. Discuss how you both honor each other's needs and what responsibilities you feel within the dynamic. This can include both emotional and physical aspects of your roles. Use this time to reflect on how your role as a submissive contributes to the power exchange and how it enriches the relationship.

    Tip: Be open and vulnerable when discussing your role, desires, and boundaries. This conversation can deepen your understanding of each other's needs and enhance your trust and connection.

    Activity 2: Exploring Power Dynamics in Daily Life
    Note how your submission fits into your daily interactions with Dominant and others. Reflect on how your role influences how you engage with the world—whether honoring your Dominant through small gestures or reflecting on how submission affects your other relationships. Embrace how this role extends beyond specific scenes and becomes a part of your everyday interactions.

Tip: Explore how your submission in daily life can be an ongoing form of devotion, respect, and connection to your Dominant. You may find that small actions, like offering a helping hand or a word of affirmation, enhance your dynamic.

Activity 3: Reflecting on Your Role as a Submissive
Take time to journal or meditate on the meaning of your role as a submissive. What does it mean to you personally? How do you feel when you embrace your submission and honor your place within the power exchange? Reflect on how this role fulfills your desires and needs and contributes to your personal growth, trust, and emotional connection.

Tip: Embrace the complexity of your role as a submissive. Understand that it involves strength and vulnerability and can lead to deep emotional and spiritual fulfillment.

- **Journaling Prompts**:

    o How does my submission enhance the power exchange in my relationship?

    o What does embracing my role in the dynamic mean to me?

    o In what ways do I honor both my own needs and the needs of my Dominant?

    o How does submission contribute to the strength and balance of our power exchange?

    o What responsibilities do I feel as a submissive, and how do they shape my actions?

Closing Reflection:

Embracing your role as a submissive within the power exchange is not just about following instructions but honoring the trust, balance, and emotional connection that bind you and your Dominant. Your submission is a source of strength, vulnerability, and devotion and is crucial to the harmonious power exchange. By understanding your role deeply and embracing it entirely, you contribute to the emotional depth and richness of the dynamic, strengthening both the relationship and your journey.

Personal Reflections:

Exploring the Duality of Control and Freedom

Meditation:

Find a comfortable space where you can relax and breathe deeply. Allow your body to settle and your mind to become present. With each inhale, feel your body relaxing more deeply into the present. With each exhale, release any tension or distractions.

Now, focus on the concept of control and freedom within your dynamic. Visualize how these two forces can exist in harmony, intertwining to create a balanced dynamic between you and your Dominant. Imagine the feeling of being in a controlled environment where your Dominant takes the lead, providing structure and direction. Feel how this sense of control offers you a safe space to surrender, trust, and let go.

As you explore this image, also notice the freedom that comes from submitting to this control. Reflect on how, in surrendering to your Dominant, you are liberated from decision-making, allowing space for personal growth, emotional release, and self-discovery. Notice how control and freedom flow together, enhancing the other, and how both can be experienced simultaneously to strengthen your emotional connection.

Affirmation:
Control and freedom coexist in harmony within our dynamic. I embrace the structure and the liberation that come with submission, knowing they work together to deepen our bond.

- **Practices in Action**:

  Activity 1: Exploring Control and Freedom Through Roleplay
  Engage in a scene where both control and freedom are explored. Perhaps your Dominant guides you through a structured task while allowing you space to choose or express yourself in specific ways. Notice how the control given to you feels like freedom in disguise, as it will enable you to make decisions within a safe, structured framework. This duality can foster trust and deepen your emotional connection.

  Tip: Communicate with your Dominant about how the balance of control and freedom feels during the scene. Be open about how each aspect influences your experience and emotional state so you both can deepen your understanding of how this balance works.

  Activity 2: Reflecting on the Experience of Control and Freedom
  After a scene, reflect on how the experience of control and freedom affected you. Were there moments when you felt fully controlled and others where you felt completely free within the structure? Consider how both elements shaped your emotional state and connection with your Dominant during the experience. Reflect on incorporating this balance more intentionally into future scenes or interactions.

Tip: Journaling about this experience can help you process the emotions and insights you gained. It can also guide future scenes, helping you better communicate your desires and needs regarding the duality of control and freedom.

Activity 3: Setting Boundaries Within Control

Explore how your submission can include freedom within the context of control by setting clear boundaries. Talk with your Dominant about what control feels empowering and where you need space for autonomy within the dynamic. Setting boundaries is essential for creating a safe environment in which to experience power and freedom. Reflect on how these boundaries can enhance your submission by allowing you to feel emotionally secure and empowered.

Tip: Establishing and honoring boundaries helps maintain a healthy dynamic, ensuring that control and freedom coexist without overshadowing the other.

- **Journaling Prompts**:

  o How does the balance of control and freedom influence my emotional state during submission?

  o What moments of freedom have I experienced within the structure of control?

  o How do I feel when my Dominant offers control and simultaneously allows space for me to make choices or express myself?

  o How can I embrace both control and freedom in a way that enhances my emotional connection with my Dominant?

  o What boundaries do I need to feel secure in control and freedom?

Closing Reflection:

The balance of control and freedom is essential to a healthy and fulfilling submission. Both elements complement and enhance each other, creating a dynamic where trust and emotional connection flourish. Control offers a sense of security and direction, while freedom within that control allows for personal growth, creativity, and emotional release. Embracing both aspects can lead to a deeper understanding of your submission and strengthen your relationship with your Dominant, creating a balanced, trusting, and nurturing dynamic.

Personal Reflections:

The Beauty of Submission as a Choice

Meditation:

Find a quiet space where you can relax deeply. Close your eyes and take a few slow, deep breaths. With each inhale, feel yourself grounded in the present moment. With each exhale, let go of any distractions or tension.

Now, focus on the power of choice within your submission. Visualize submission not as a duty or obligation but as a conscious and empowered decision. Reflect on the strength of submitting actively and how that choice can be a source of joy, freedom, and connection. Feel the weight of that decision, not as something forced, but as something you give willingly, knowing it leads to deeper trust, intimacy, and understanding with your Dominant.

Consider how this choice enhances your sense of self and relationship with your Dominant. Submission, as a choice, means that you are always in control of your surrender, giving of yourself in trust and love. Reflect on how this conscious choice enhances the depth of your submission and empowers you within the dynamic.

Affirmation:
My submission is a conscious, empowered choice. I embrace it fully, knowing that in choosing to submit, I strengthen our connection and deepen my sense of self.

- **Practices in Action**:

  Activity 1: Reaffirming Your Choice
  Take a moment to reaffirm your choice to submit consciously. You can do this through a simple act of dedication or an inner affirmation. This could be through a ritual, a moment of stillness, or a verbal affirmation with your Dominant. Reaffirming your choice reminds you and your dominance of the power in your submission, strengthening the emotional foundation of your dynamic.

  Tip: Communicate to your Dominant how important this conscious choice is to you. Let them know how reaffirming your decision to submit makes you feel empowered and connected.

  Activity 2: Exploring the Joy of Submission
  When chosen freely, submission can bring a deep sense of joy and fulfillment. Explore a scene or activity where you fully embrace the joy of submission. This could be as simple as serving your Dominant or as profound as fully surrendering in a deeply connected, vulnerable moment. Please pay attention to how it feels to be in the space of active, joyful submission and notice the emotional release it provides.

  Tip: Notice the moments of joy that arise from your submission. These can often be subtle but profoundly impactful. Acknowledge these moments and share them with your Dominant to help deepen your connection.

Activity 3: Reflecting on Empowerment Through Choice
After a scene or interaction, take time to reflect on how it felt to choose submission consciously. How did this choice affect your emotional state during the experience? Consider how embracing your submission as a choice has empowered you within the dynamic. What aspects of this conscious decision do you appreciate most, and how does it enhance your connection with your Dominant?

Tip: Journaling about your experience can help solidify your understanding of how submission as a choice impacts your emotional and mental well-being and the relationship dynamics.

- **Journaling Prompts**:

    o How does consciously choosing to submit empower me within the dynamic?

    o What moments during submission remind me of the strength of my choice?

    o How do I feel when I reaffirm my decision to submit?

    o In what ways does my submission bring joy, both to me and my Dominant?

    o How does choosing submission affect my sense of control and freedom within the relationship?

Closing Reflection:

Submission is a powerful choice, not done out of obligation or expectation but as a conscious, loving decision to surrender in trust and connection. When submission is approached as a choice, it becomes an empowering act, deepening the bond between you and your Dominant. This choice fosters trust, freedom, and joy, creating a foundation of respect and mutual understanding within the dynamic. By consciously choosing to submit, you embrace the beauty of that surrender, knowing it brings personal growth and a deeper connection to your Dominant.

Personal Reflections:

The Importance of Self-Awareness in Submission

Meditation:

Find a quiet space where you can relax comfortably. Take several deep breaths, grounding yourself in the present moment. With each inhale, feel a sense of calm and centeredness; with each exhale, release any tension or distractions.

Now, focus on your inner world. Reflect on how your emotions, thoughts, and desires influence your submission experience. How do your personal feelings—whether of joy, vulnerability, discomfort, or fulfillment—shape the way you engage in submission? Take time to understand the deeper layers of your emotions and how they connect to your willingness to submit. How do these emotions impact your trust, boundaries, and connection to your Dominant?

Think about the importance of self-awareness in submission. Understanding your needs, triggers, and desires helps you navigate the dynamic authentically and clearly. The more aware you are of your emotional landscape, the more you can communicate with your Dominant and create a space for deeper connection and mutual respect.

Affirmation:
In my submission, I honor my emotions and cultivate self-awareness. By understanding myself, I deepen my trust and connection with my Dominant.

- **Practices in Action**:

  Activity 1: Journaling Your Emotions After a Scene
  After a scene or meaningful interaction, spend some time journaling about your emotions. How did you feel before, during, and after the experience? Reflect on any feelings that arose, such as joy, fear, excitement, vulnerability, or discomfort. Notice if there were any surprises or insights about yourself during the interaction. Journaling helps you process your emotions and develop greater self-awareness about how submission affects you.

  Tip: Focus not only on the surface emotions but also on the deeper layers. Consider how your emotions relate to past experiences, personal needs, or desires. If you feel comfortable, share these reflections with your Dominant to deepen your mutual understanding.

  Activity 2: Checking In with Your Feelings Before a Scene
  Before engaging in a scene, take a moment to check in with yourself emotionally. How do you feel about the upcoming experience? Do you want to express any concerns, desires, or emotional needs? Checking in with your emotions before a scene helps you stay aligned with your boundaries and desires, ensuring the experience is fulfilling and respectful.

  Tip: Communicate your emotional state openly with your Dominant, even if it's just a simple acknowledgment of your emotional well-being. This helps you stay connected and aware of each other's emotional needs.

Activity 3: Reflecting on Self-Awareness in the Dynamic

After reflecting on and journaling about your emotions, consider how self-awareness has influenced your submission. How has being more in tune with your feelings helped you navigate your submission? Consider how this awareness has deepened your connection, trust, and communication ability with your Dominant.

Tip: Share these reflections with your Dominant to better understand each other's emotional needs and boundaries. This can help strengthen your dynamic and enhance the emotional depth of your submission.

- **Journaling Prompts**:

    o What emotions arise for me before, during, and after submission?

    o How do my feelings of vulnerability, trust, or joy shape my submission?

    o How has being aware of my emotional state improved my communication with my Dominant?

    o What are the deeper emotional needs I have that I want to express in submission?

    o How does self-awareness in submission help me set and honor my boundaries?

Closing Reflection:

Self-awareness is a powerful tool in submission. By understanding your emotions, desires, and boundaries, you not only navigate submission with greater clarity but also enhance the depth of your connection with your Dominant. Self-awareness allows for more authentic communication, deeper trust, and mutual respect, creating a safe and fulfilling dynamic. Through self-reflection and understanding, submission becomes a process of emotional discovery, where you and your Dominant grow and evolve together.

Personal Reflections:

Exploring Emotional Reactions to Discipline

Meditation:

Find a quiet space to relax and reflect. Take several deep breaths, feeling your body release any tension with each exhale. Ground yourself in the present moment and center your mind.

Now, focus on the emotional responses that arise regarding discipline or correction. Reflect on the different feelings you might experience—such as guilt, relief, gratitude, frustration, or even vulnerability. How do you feel before, during, and after discipline takes place? Consider how discipline serves as guidance in your dynamic and what emotional reactions it stirs within you.

Think about how discipline, when done with care, can deepen trust and reinforce the connection between you and your Dominant. How does your emotional response to discipline reflect your understanding of your role within the dynamic? Does it strengthen your submission or challenge you to confront and process certain emotions?

Affirmation:
I embrace the discipline within my dynamic as a pathway to growth, trust, and deeper connection. I accept correction with an open heart and a willingness to learn.

- **Practices in Action**:

  Activity 1: Discussing the Role of Discipline
  Have an open conversation with your Dominant about how discipline plays a role in your dynamic. What does discipline mean to both of you and how do you perceive it emotionally? Discuss your feelings about discipline, how it's handled, and its impact on your submission. Sharing these feelings can help you better understand each other's needs and emotional responses.

  Tip: Approach this conversation with openness and vulnerability, allowing space for an honest discussion about what discipline means to you personally and how it affects your emotional connection with your Dominant.

  Activity 2: Exploring Emotional Responses in Real Time
  After disciplinary action, take a moment to check in with your emotional state. How do you feel after the discipline? Are there any specific emotions that arise, such as relief, tension, or confusion? Take time to reflect on these emotions and process them in the moment.

  Tip: If you feel comfortable, share these emotions with your Dominant. Express how the discipline impacted you and discuss any lingering feelings or thoughts. This can help you both grow in understanding and build a stronger emotional connection.

  Activity 3: Reflecting on Growth Through Discipline
  After some time following a disciplinary moment, reflect on how it has

impacted your submission and growth. Do you feel closer to your Dominant after being corrected? Has the experience changed your emotional connection or deepened your trust? Reflecting on how the discipline has contributed to your personal growth can be a way to honor both your submission and your Dominant's role.

Tip: Focus on how discipline helps you become more self-aware, strengthening your submission over time. Acknowledge the lessons learned and how they enhance your relationship's emotional depth and growth.

- **Journaling Prompts**:

  - How do I emotionally react to discipline? What feelings arise in me before, during, and after a disciplinary moment?

  - What does discipline mean to me within my submission? How does it help me grow emotionally and mentally?

  - How do I feel about the way my Dominant handles discipline?

  - How has discipline deepened my emotional connection with my Dominant?

  - What role does trust play in my emotional response to discipline?

Closing Reflection:

Discipline is essential to healthy, dynamic submission, offering structure and guidance. Your emotional responses reflect how deeply submission intertwines with your emotional life. By embracing discipline with openness and understanding, you allow greater trust and connection to blossom in your relationship. You and your Dominant can grow through disciplined moments, deepening your emotional bond and creating a more vital, resilient dynamic. When handled with care, discipline fosters growth and reinforces submission as a powerful, transformative journey.

Personal Reflections:

Celebrating Your Growth Through Submission

Meditation:

Find a quiet space to sit comfortably and take several deep breaths. Allow your body to relax with each exhale and feel your mind settling into the present moment.

Now, reflect on your journey as a submissive. Visualize the growth you've made, both emotionally and mentally. Think about the challenges you've faced, the moments of vulnerability you've embraced, and the strength you've found in your submission. Picture yourself standing at the culmination of this growth, proud of the person you've become. What lessons have you learned through your submission, and how have they transformed you?

Consider how your submission has deepened your connection with your Dominant and yourself. Reflect on how each moment of submission—each act of surrender—has allowed you to grow, evolve, and become more self-aware. Embrace the pride in knowing your submission is a powerful, personal journey that brings growth and connection.

Affirmation:
Through submission, I celebrate my growth and transformation. I honor the lessons I've learned and the strength I've gained. My submission is a journey of empowerment, trust, and connection.

- **Practices in Action:**

  Activity 1: Reflecting on Key Moments of Growth
  Reflect on specific moments in your journey as a submissive where you've experienced personal growth. Was there a moment when you learned to embrace vulnerability? A time when you overcame a fear or boundary? Share these experiences with your Dominant, focusing on how each moment has shaped your submission. Celebrate your progress together, recognizing how your growth strengthens the dynamic.

  Tip: When sharing your growth, emphasize how the experience impacted you and your Dominant. Celebrate the collaborative journey you've both been on and how it's enriched your submission and connection.

  Activity 2: Acknowledging Your Strengths
  Identify the strengths you've gained through your submission. How has submission helped you become more self-aware, compassionate, or empowered? Please write down your strengths and reflect on how they have influenced your submission. Share these insights with your Dominant, acknowledging both the strength in your submission and the power you've cultivated within yourself.

Tip: Focus on the positive aspects of your submission and how it has impacted your self-esteem and emotional well-being. This activity is an opportunity to celebrate who you are becoming due to your submission.

Activity 3: Celebrating the Journey Together
Take time to celebrate your submission journey with your Dominant. Plan a moment or ritual where both of you can acknowledge and honor the progress you've made as a team. This could involve a particular conversation, a symbolic gesture, or a simple moment of gratitude. The celebration should reflect the significance of your shared growth and the strength of your bond.

Tip: Focus on honoring both your individual growth and your shared connection. This celebration isn't just about personal achievements; it's also about the partnership that has allowed you to evolve and grow together.

- **Journaling Prompts**:

    o What critical moments in my submission journey are I most proud of?

    o How has my submission transformed me emotionally, mentally, or spiritually?

    o What strengths have I gained through submission that I am most proud of?

    o How has my submission deepened my connection with my Dominant?

    o In what ways have I overcome challenges in my submission, and how do I feel about those experiences?

    o How do I want to celebrate my progress and growth within my submission journey?

Closing Reflection:

Submission is about surrender and the robust growth that comes with it. Each step along the way—each act of vulnerability, trust, and surrender—has the potential to shape and transform you. By taking the time to celebrate your growth, you honor the progress you've made and the strength you've gained. Submission is a personal growth journey, and recognizing your achievements brings a more profound sense of pride, trust, and connection. Together, with your Dominant, celebrate the beautiful journey you are on and the profound growth that continues to unfold.

Personal Reflections:

Balancing Your Submission with Personal Strength

Meditation:

Find a quiet, comfortable space to relax and clear your mind. Take a deep breath, inhaling slowly and exhaling gently, feeling your body settle into a calm state.

Now, reflect on the balance between your submission and your power. Submission is often seen as surrendering control but can coexist with your inner strength and independence. Visualize how these two aspects of yourself—your submission and your power—work together harmoniously, creating a balanced and empowered dynamic. Consider how your submission allows you to embrace vulnerability while honoring your ability to stand firm in your personal beliefs, boundaries, and desires.

Think about how submission doesn't diminish your strength but enhances it. Your willingness to submit is a conscious choice that reflects confidence and trust in yourself and your Dominant. You are not giving up your power but sharing it in a way that fosters deeper connection and growth. Let yourself feel the strength of balancing both submission and personal empowerment.

Affirmation:
My submission is an expression of my inner strength. I honor my power while embracing the growth that submission brings. My submission enhances my autonomy and my connection with my Dominant.

- **Practices in Action**:

    Activity 1: Understanding Your Boundaries
    Take time to reflect on the boundaries that define your strength. You draw these lines regarding emotional, mental, and physical well-being. Share these boundaries with your Dominant, emphasizing how they support your ability to maintain strength within the dynamic. Reflect on how setting and honoring boundaries enhances your submission and empowerment.

    Tip: Remember, submission is a conscious choice; part of that choice involves knowing where your limits lie. Discussing these boundaries with your Dominant ensures that your submission always aligns with your strength.

    Activity 2: Exploring Your Independence Within Submission
    Reflect on areas where you maintain independence while in a submissive dynamic. It could be in your career, friendships, or personal development. Discuss these aspects with your Dominant, focusing on how your independence and submission coexist. Identify ways your Dominant supports your autonomy, allowing you to grow as an individual while nurturing your submission.

    Tip: Submission's dynamic should empower you to be your best self. When supported by the submission, independence creates a more fulfilling and balanced experience.

Activity 3: Recognizing Strength in Submission
Reflect on times when you've felt powerful in your submission. Perhaps it was in a moment of surrender or when you maintained your boundaries while still submitting. Share these moments with your Dominant, exploring how submission can be a source of strength rather than weakness. Recognizing these moments can help reinforce the understanding that your submission is an empowered choice.

Tip: Take pride in moments where your submission aligns with your strength. It's a testament to your growth and the balance you've achieved within the dynamic.

- **Journaling Prompts**:

    o   How does submission enhance my strength and independence?

    o   In what ways do I feel empowered by my submission?

    o   How do my boundaries help me balance submission with my inner strength?

    o   What moments have my submission journey shown me that submission and strength coexist?

    o   How can I further integrate my independence into my submission dynamic?

    o   How does my submission allow me to embrace vulnerability and personal power?

Closing Reflection:

Balancing submission with personal strength is an ongoing journey. Submission is not relinquishing power but a conscious act of trust, surrender, and mutual respect. By understanding and honoring your strength, you can create a dynamic where submission enhances your sense of self, allowing you to grow individually and within the relationship. When submission is balanced with personal empowerment, it becomes a source of strength and transformation for you and your Dominant, fostering deeper trust, respect, and connection.

Personal Reflections:

Exploring the Role of Rituals in Deepening Submission

Meditation:

Find a peaceful space to sit or lie down comfortably. Take deep, steady breaths, allowing your mind to clear with each exhale. As you relax, envision the role of ritual in your submission.

Imagine the power of a ritual, a consistent and intentional act that brings more profound meaning and connection to your dynamic with your Dominant. Visualize how performing a ritual, whether physical or emotional, enhances your submission, allowing it to flow naturally with purpose and intent. Think of a ritual that brings you a sense of devotion and connection, strengthening your bond.

Feel the presence of your Dominant as they guide you through this ritual, and reflect on how such an act reinforces your trust, devotion, and submission. A ritual can be an intimate practice that grounds you, strengthens your role, and deepens your submission's emotional and spiritual aspects.

Affirmation:
Rituals in my submission deepen my trust and devotion to my Dominant. Each ritual brings me closer to my true self and strengthens our emotional and spiritual connection.

- **Practices in Action**:

    Activity 1: Creating Your Ritual
    Consider a ritual that speaks to you—a way to honor your submission and deepen your connection. It might be a morning ritual that sets the tone for your day, a ritual before or after scenes, or a moment of reflection shared between you and your Dominant. Think about elements such as words, actions, or gestures that feel significant.

    When you've envisioned your ritual, please share it with your Dominant and ask for their input. Together, decide how this ritual can be integrated into your dynamic to strengthen your emotional connection and reaffirm your submission.

    Tip: The ritual doesn't have to be elaborate; even small, meaningful gestures can carry deep significance in reinforcing your submission.

    Activity 2: Participating in a Ritual Together
    Explore how you can create or engage in rituals that honor the dynamic. This could be a recurring practice that you both enjoy and find meaningful, such as specific words or actions performed during scenes or times of reflection. Rituals don't have to be ceremonial—they can also be simple acts that mark significant moments of connection, such as serving your Dominant in a specific way or engaging in an affirming conversation.

Tip: Rituals should reflect the energy and intention of your dynamic, fostering an environment where submission and connection thrive.

Activity 3: Journaling About Rituals and Submission

After practicing a ritual, take time to journal about the experience. What emotions and thoughts arose during the ritual? Did the ritual deepen your feelings of submission, trust, or devotion? Reflect on how the ritual affects your relationship with your Dominant and how it strengthens your submission.

Tip: Journaling can deepen your understanding of how rituals affect your submission and allow you to track your emotional and spiritual growth over time.

- **Journaling Prompts**:

    - How does a ritual enhance my sense of submission to my Dominant?

    - What rituals, big or small, help deepen my connection with my Dominant?

    - How do rituals affect my emotional and spiritual growth within the dynamic?

    - What feelings arise when I engage in a ritual reaffirming my submission?

    - How can I create rituals that honor and strengthen my devotion to my Dominant?

    - What significance do rituals have in the overall experience of submission?

Closing Reflection:

Rituals hold a special place in the submission dynamic, offering a way to reflect, reaffirm, and deepen the connection with your Dominant. These practices enhance the emotional bond and the spiritual and psychological aspects of submission. Through rituals, submission becomes a conscious, meaningful choice, creating moments of trust, reverence, and devotion. As you explore and develop rituals, allow them to be a source of grounding, a reminder of your strength and submission, and a powerful way to honor your role and your Dominant's.

Personal Reflections:

The Importance of Clear Communication in Submission

Meditation:

Find a comfortable position where you can relax and focus your mind. Take a few deep breaths, letting your body release tension with each exhale. As you settle into the moment, reflect on the importance of communication within your role as a submissive.

Visualize a transparent, open line of communication between you and your Dominant, where words are spoken freely, honestly, and without fear of judgment. Think about how powerful communication is within your submission: it allows your Dominant to understand your needs, desires, and boundaries. It helps you express your emotional state and personal growth, creating a safe space for both of you to thrive.

Consider how clear communication strengthens your relationship, enhances trust, and deepens your connection. Reflect on moments where good communication has led to a more fulfilling dynamic and where miscommunication has created challenges.

Affirmation:

Clear, open communication is the foundation of my submission. It creates trust, understanding, and emotional depth in my dynamic with my Dominant.

- **Practices in Action**:

    Activity 1: Open Discussion with Your Dominant
    Set aside time for a calm, uninterrupted conversation with your Dominant. This conversation should focus on your needs, desires, and boundaries. Be honest about what you need from the dynamic, what brings you fulfillment, and what might be difficult for you. This practice will allow both of you to have a deeper understanding of each other and learn how to support each other in the best relationship.

    Tip: Approach the conversation with an open heart and mind, ready to listen and express yourself. Communication is a two-way process.

    Activity 2: Share Your Limits and Desires Clearly
    Practice being transparent with your Dominant about your boundaries and desires. It might feel vulnerable, but expressing your limits and needs is essential to maintaining a healthy dynamic. Be clear about what you are comfortable with and where your boundaries lie, and also share what you are excited about or curious to explore. The more you communicate, the easier it will be to navigate your dynamic together.

    Tip: Regularly check in with your Dominant to ensure your communication stays open and fluid. This fosters mutual respect and understanding.

Activity 3: Reflect on Your Communication Style

Take time to reflect on your communication style. Are you clear and assertive about your boundaries? Are there areas where you could improve in expressing your needs or emotions? Consider how your communication style may have evolved and what steps you can take to enhance it further. Understanding how you communicate helps to strengthen your submission by ensuring you are heard and understood.

Tip: If you struggle with communication, consider journaling or seeking guidance on expressing yourself more openly and confidently.

- **Journaling Prompts**:

  - How has clear communication improved my submission experience?

  - What role does communication play in creating a safe and trusting space within my dynamic?

  - How do I feel when I express my desires and boundaries openly to my Dominant?

  - What challenges have I faced in communicating my needs, and how can I address them?

  - How can I ensure that my Dominant understands my emotional and physical limits?

  - How does communication enhance my emotional connection and submission?

  - What steps can I take to improve communication in my dynamic?

Closing Reflection:

Clear and open communication is vital for a healthy and fulfilling submission dynamic. It ensures that you and your Dominant understand each other's needs and desires, fostering a sense of trust, respect, and emotional connection. Being transparent about your boundaries and emotions creates a foundation of safety and mutual understanding that strengthens your submission. Remember that communication is an ongoing process, and checking in with each other regularly is essential to maintain a robust and fulfilling dynamic.

Personal Reflections:

Celebrating Your Submission as a Source of Power

Meditation:

Find a peaceful space where you can sit comfortably and focus inward. Take several deep breaths, releasing tension in your body with each exhale. As you begin to relax, reflect on how submission is not a weakness but, in fact, a unique and profound source of strength and power.

Visualize your submission as radiant energy flowing from within you, connecting you to your Dominant, your true self, and a deeper level of understanding and trust. See your submission as a courageous and empowering act demonstrating your ability to surrender to the process and honor your role in the dynamic.

Think about how submission allows you to fully embrace your desires, trust in the guidance of your Dominant, and experience growth in ways you may not have imagined. Submission does not make you powerless; it highlights your inner strength, vulnerability, and commitment. Reflect on how, through submission, you can fully express your emotional depth, resilience, and devotion.

Affirmation:
My submission is a source of power and strength. Through it, I discovered my true self and grew in ways I never thought possible.

- **Practices in Action**:

  Activity 1: Affirm Your Submission
  Stand in front of a mirror or find a quiet place where you feel at peace. With conviction, say out loud: "My submission is a powerful gift. It brings me closer to my true self and deepens my connection with my Dominant." Repeat this affirmation several times, feeling the words resonate within you. Let the affirmation strengthen your sense of power through submission and remind you that it is a beautiful choice, full of purpose and strength.

  Tip: Practice saying this affirmation regularly to reinforce your belief in your submission as a source of empowerment.

  Activity 2: Acknowledge the Strength of Your Submission
  Take a moment to reflect on the areas where your submission has demonstrated personal strength. How have you handled difficult situations with grace and trust? How has submission helped you grow in resilience and emotional maturity? Share this with your Dominant, acknowledging how submission has shaped you into a stronger, more confident person.

  Tip: Recognizing your growth and strength can help shift perceptions of submission as a weakness. Celebrate the courage it takes to submit fully.

  Activity 3: Embrace the Power of Surrender
  Submission often requires surrender—letting go of control and trusting your

Dominant's guidance. This act of surrender is a powerful form of strength. Engage in a scene or practice where you surrender completely, allowing your Dominant to take charge, and reflect on how it feels to be so fully immersed in trust and vulnerability. Notice the inner strength you possess in such moments of surrender.

Tip: Let yourself feel empowered by your ability to trust, surrender, and submit—acknowledge that this is a powerful act of personal strength.

- **Journaling Prompts**:

    o   In what ways has submission empowered me in my relationship?

    o   How does submission allow me to explore new dimensions of my strength?

    o   When I surrender, what strength do I find in letting go of control?

    o   How has my submission shaped my ability to trust and be vulnerable?

    o   How does submission create space for personal growth and development?

    o   What moments in my dynamic have reminded me of the power within my submission?

    o   How can I celebrate the strength of my submission in my life?

Closing Reflection:

Submission is a powerful act that requires inner strength, vulnerability, and trust. It is a conscious choice to surrender control to embrace a deeper connection with your Dominant and with yourself. Rather than diminishing your power, submission enhances your ability to embrace your desires, grow emotionally, and discover new levels of personal strength. Recognize that submission is not about weakness but about choosing to trust, give, and fully experience life with purpose and intention.

Personal Reflections:

Embracing the Strength in Submission

As we reach the final pages of this exploration, we take a moment to reflect on everything that has been shared, explored, and experienced throughout your journey in submission. Your path is one of deep self-awareness, emotional richness, and profound connection with your Dominant. But more than that, it's been a journey of embracing the beautiful paradox that submission embodies—where strength and vulnerability, control and surrender, power and trust intertwine to create something uniquely empowering.

Submission is not about weakness, nor is it about being passive. It is an active, conscious choice that requires trust, strength, and deep self-awareness. Throughout this guide, you've explored how submission can be a powerful tool for personal growth, healing, and deepening emotional connections. Whether surrendering to your Dominant's guidance, expressing your desires, or honoring your boundaries, submission is an act of courage and self-expression.

Through each meditation, practice, and journaling prompt, you've been invited to uncover the nuances of your submission, explore what it means to submit with the agency, and discover how your vulnerability can be one of your greatest strengths. Submission is not a surrender of your power but rather an embrace of a different kind of power—one that comes from trusting, giving, and sharing in a dynamic of mutual respect, care, and devotion.

As you reflect on your journey, remember that submission, when done consciously, is a choice that can elevate you. It can bring you closer to your most authentic self, amplify your emotional growth, and foster an environment of deep intimacy and connection with your Dominant. It allows you to release control and trust in another person and explore new dimensions of pleasure, trust, and emotional fulfillment. In these spaces of trust and surrender, you can discover profound emotional catharsis, personal empowerment, and growth.

One of the most beautiful aspects of submission is how it navigates the delicate dance between power and surrender. Submission allows you to explore your relationship with power—not as something to wield, but as something to give away freely and receive gracefully. You've learned that submission is not about being powerless. Instead, it is about consciously entering a dynamic where power exchange leads to deeper trust, fulfillment, and connection.

You've also learned to embrace your power within the dynamic as you've practiced surrendering. Whether you've explored silence, communication, emotional release, or discipline, every step has brought you closer to the realization that submission is a powerful choice that comes from knowing your desires, acknowledging your needs, and trusting in your Dominant's guidance. It's a space where you can express strength and vulnerability without fear of judgment, knowing that each part of you—every desire, every boundary, and every need—is worthy of being expressed, seen, and respected.

The foundation of trust, respect, and open communication lies at the heart of every successful dynamic. Without these elements, submission can quickly become a discomfort rather than an empowerment space. Through this guide, you've been encouraged to communicate openly with your Dominant, to set boundaries, and to express your desires with clarity and honesty. You've learned that submission isn't just passive—it's about taking an active role in your dynamic, being transparent about your needs, and continuously exploring how you can grow together.

By engaging in these practices, you've also learned to trust yourself and that your desires, needs, and feelings matter. And just as importantly, you've learned to trust your Dominant, knowing they will honor your boundaries and guide you in ways that encourage growth, exploration, and deep connection.

As you reflect on all you've discovered, it's time to celebrate. Every step of this journey has brought you closer to understanding the depths of your submission and discovering how it can be a source of strength, connection, and power. You've allowed yourself to explore your desires, confront fears, embrace challenges, and experience the profound joys of submitting consciously and confidently.

In this final chapter of your exploration, I encourage you to celebrate everything you've learned. Celebrate the moments of vulnerability, the deepening trust, the emotional release, and the strength you've discovered within yourself. Submission is not about perfection. It's about the willingness to grow, to be open, and to trust the process. It's about knowing that each moment—each act of submission—adds to your personal growth, connection, and power.

As you close this book and take these lessons into your life and dynamic, remember that submission is not about losing yourself. Instead, it's about discovering parts of you that you might not have known existed—strengths, desires, and emotions that come to light when you allow yourself to trust, give, and submit. The joy of submission comes from the profound connection you create with your Dominant, the emotional growth you experience, and the trust that deepens with each step.

In a world that often misunderstands submission as a weakness, we know the truth: submission is an act of deep inner strength. It is the power to surrender, trust, and choose to give of yourself in a way that brings you closer to your true self and dominance. It is a choice to engage in the sacred dance of vulnerability and trust, embrace your chosen role, and celebrate the strength in letting go.

Now, take these lessons with you. Continue exploring, growing, and deepening your connection. And remember: each moment you choose to submit is a celebration of the power within you.

You've come so far on this journey. Take what you've learned and continue to explore, grow, and thrive in your submission. The cuffs may come off when the time is right, but the strength, trust, and deep connection you've cultivated will always be there—ready to lead you into the next chapter of your journey.